D0601713

The
GAME

The GAME

★ ★ ★

Win Your Life
in 90 Days

Sarano Kelley

Jodere Group, Inc.
San Diego, California

Copyright © 2001 by Sarano Kelley

Published by: Jodere Group, Inc., P.O. Box 910147, San Diego, CA 92191-0147 • (800) 569-1002

Distributed in the United States by: Hay House, Inc., P.O. Box 5100, Carlsbad, CA 92018-5100 • (800) 654-5126 • (800) 650-5115 (fax) • www.hayhouse.com

All rights reserved. No part of this book may be reproduced by any mechanical, photographic, or electronic process, or in the form of a phonographic recording; nor may it be stored in a retrieval system, transmitted, or otherwise be copied for public or private use—other than for "fair use" as brief quotations embodied in articles and reviews without prior written permission of the publisher.

The author of this book does not dispense medical advice or prescribe the use of any technique as a form of treatment for physical or medical problems without the advice of a physician, either directly or indirectly. The intent of the author is only to offer information of a general nature to help you in your quest for emotional and spiritual well-being. In the event you use any of the information in this book for yourself, which is your constitutional right, the author and the publisher assume no responsibility for your actions.

Library of Congress Cataloging-in-Publication Data

Kelley, Sarano.
    The game : win your life in 90 days / Sarano Kelley.
        p. cm.
    ISBN 1-58872-004-7
    1. Success. 2. Conduct of life. I. Title.

BJ1611 .K45 2001
158--dc21

                                                        00-065511

ISBN 1-58872-004-7

04 03 02 01   4 3 2 1
1st printing, April 2001

Printed in the United States of America

★ ★ ★

*Dedicated
to my father*

★ ★ ★

Contents

★ ★ ★

✶ Acknowledgments ✶

There are more people I owe an acknowledgment to than there are pages in this book. I'd like to thank all of them, as well as all of you who are contributing by reading this book, so my list grows longer by the moment. However, I would be remiss to at least not try to do some justice to so many of the people who have made this possible.

First, I want to thank my mother and father. Never have I had two stronger supporters than these two. I consider it an honor to be their son. My brother, Janaria, and my sister, Arketa, also made this book possible through their amazing selfless service, as well as that of their families.

My second father came in the form of a great man and teacher, Mr. Leon McClaren, and his protégé and my most immediate teacher, Mr. Barry Steingard. They took a somewhat promising young man and gave me the stillness and direction to put my dreams into action.

I offer a special thanks for the combined wisdom and opportunity granted to me by Mark Sutton of Paine Webber, and Barbara Brooks, Gail Wickes, and Steve Goddard.

Jack Sharry of Phoenix Investment Partners and Chairman Bob Fiondella pushed me out of my comfortable small circle of clients and made me get on the platform to explain what I had learned to the world.

My gratitude goes to Dr. Martin Kettelhut for being my constant companion on this journey, and co-founder with me of **TheCoachingProgram.com.**

I'm grateful for the friendship and business acumen of master coaches Ken Doyle, R.W. "Butch" Nicholson, and Gino Copolla; and to our staff members Kim Thomas, Lauren Eichner-Forsee, Leslie Nelson, and Carrie Leavenworth, who threw their lives into serving others through their work with **TheCoachingProgram.com.**

When I met Arielle Ford, my agent and publicist and one of the greatest ladies of my life, and her incredible husband, Brian Hilliard, also my agent, their agencies Dharma Dreams and Ford Group became my global dream makers. They immediately and continually believed in me and will forever be my friends. Arielle and Brian introduced me to my wonderful publisher, Debbie Luican.

A special thanks to The Center for Excellence's founders and original supporters: Allen Dogger, Bill Meyer, Bruce Bjerke, R.W. Butch Nicholson, Christopher Sutton, Cindy Tercha, Cynthia Komarek, Dean Lampe, Don Berryman, Ed Dawson, Eric Bodner, Jordan C. Meyer and R. Henry Meyer, Kay Copley, Ken Doyle, Kenneth Bingham, Lou Valli, Mary Wichmann, Michael Haynes, Mike Golub, Orville Lerch, Phil Economopolis, Rhonda Finby, Sally Vail, Sean Hattrick, Tom Aylmer, Tommy Goodrum, Tony Milburn, and William Zalewski.

I sincerely appreciate the support and advice of TCE Associates, L.L.C.'s senior board of advisors: Laura Goldzung, Bob Seaberg, Jim Marrin, Rich Franchella, Barbara Brooks, Linda Munn, Laura Lange, Don Conolley, Mikhail Lapushner, Stu Veale, Jack Sharry, Mark Warren, Delynn Copely, Richard Kaye, Peter Janssen, Ted Fuller, and my business advisor and friend, Marty Beaulieu.

In addition, I greatly appreciate the excellent work from **TheGameInteractive.com's** technology team: Ian Gardner, Paulynn Cue and Tim Donner.

Special thanks to everyone who allowed me to use a quote or story for this book. Your courage, honesty, and honor make you real trailblazers.

The writer who helped me with this book, Linda Anderson (a.k.a. "The Oracle"), cracks the most loving whip I've ever had the pleasure of working under, and her brilliance illuminates every page.

Last, I would like to thank my partner, Christine Kelley—who was always there when I needed a friend—for giving me the greatest gift of my life: our daughter, Georgia Blaze Kelley.

✶ ✶ ✶

✦ INTRODUCTION ✦

When will your real life happen?

Groping for the off-button on your alarm clock, drowning traffic noises with the cackling of morning radio hosts, checking e-mail and filtering through stacks of phone messages at work, picking up groceries for that diet you've been wanting to start, making the kids finish their homework, slipping into bed after the evening news, and wearily setting the alarm for the next day—this can't be your real life. This isn't the life you described when adults used to ask you what you wanted to be when you grew up. Your real life must have taken a detour along the way from childhood to maturity.

You mislaid your real life. It's been lost in the mail. Now where *did* you put it? Your real life is waiting like an unopened gift you threw into the back of your closet and forgot about. Your real life is buried under ordinariness, busy-ness, and unfulfilled dreams. Your real life plans to show up. Someday.

After all your obligations are met.

After the children have been raised and have left home. After those investments pay off big-time.

Later.

Will "Later" Ever Get Here?

"Later" is a very sneaky opponent to living your real life. It's always convincing you that whatever needs to be done will somehow be improved by waiting. How many moments are accumulating into years while you put off until later those things you've always wanted to do? We defer not only our big goals, but also put off showing kindness, getting help for ourselves, telling people we love them, or taking up a hobby.

As we get older, we do our best to make sure that everything stays the same. We drive the same way every day when going to work. We eat the same foods at the same restaurants; we make love to the same music and by the same glow of candlelight. We lose vitality, enjoyment, and newness in life and relationships. We're human beings who have been caught in a dream and are sleepwalking through our lives.

Did you know that some people wake up and take a different course? They find extraordinary powers within themselves. Awakened dreamers accomplish goals beyond their imaginations. They become heroes and examples for us all.

You can fulfill the dreams and promises you made to yourself. You can accomplish all the important things you ever wanted to do in your life. All you have to do is wholeheartedly play a *game*—but not the type of game you've been playing where you procrastinate and give yourself excuses.

The system I've designed and call *The Game* is an operating manual for your life to give you a structure for accomplishing your highest aspirations in only 90 days. And, yes, it's an actual game with players, fans, time limits, coaches, competition, cooperation, and prizes. For 15 years, I've taught The Game's technology to more than 250,000 busy, wealthy, successful, and stressed-out people. They've applied my proven technology to break old habits, create new ones, and use their natural abilities more fully. Many have told me that in only 90 days they've produced extraordinary results by expanding from using an estimated 5 to 10 percent of their resources to operating at 80 to 100 percent capacity. This is why I say that The Game helps you *win* your life. It's a quest for the life you've always wanted—the life you've been waiting for and hoping would happen someday.

Now Instead of Later

Many people don't expect to optimally enjoy life until retirement, yet some retirees die shortly after leaving their jobs. Later. It just doesn't work out the way we thought it would.

When I was a child, I didn't believe in this *later* nonsense. The superhuman powers of fictional heroes in comic books I loved to read—Batman, Superman, and the X-Men—convinced me that anything was possible *right now*. Their adventures stimulated my imagination and inspired me to explore the limits of what I could do and be.

Like most young people who enter the world of work, family, and responsibility, I quickly forgot that I'd ever thought mere mortals could achieve the daring feats of science-fiction characters. I no longer believed that, like the superheroes I admired, I could make my life into anything I wanted it to be. Playing The Game changed all of that for me. I learned that I didn't have to defer my life to some later day or wait to become more of what I'd always wanted to be.

What Is The Game?

The Game is completely made up. Even though playing it could make an enormous difference in your life, the good news is that you have a 50-50 chance of succeeding because you either play it or you don't.

The Game helps you find the richness in daily life, in the present—not at some future time or by increasing the number of your possessions. The Game teaches you that you've been a master manipulator of yourself. All those promises you've made, the things you could have done but never did—you probably weren't ever going to get around to doing them. If you could have, you would have. Instead, you've turned your life toward contraction instead of expansion. The Game puts you in exactly the opposite direction because, by its very nature, it's focused on expansiveness. You play The Game even though you think your life is fine, thank you, just the way it is.

The playing field for The Game is your own life. In this book, I'll give you the information you'll need to accomplish whatever you want. My goal is to help you get to be more like *you*, not more like me or others who have played The Game. You import The Game into your own life and adapt it to your circumstances. Each Game is uniquely tailored to the individual, because *you* are the player of your own life. No two Games are alike. The Game is entirely subjective, just as our perceptions of reality mean that no two people, not even identical twins, look at life in exactly the same way.

This is unlike any self-help book you've read because it can be a companion to any school of thought that appeals to you. I'll be offering you examples and information to inspire you, but I encourage you not to wait until your next crisis hits to start applying what you're learning in this book. If you follow my instructions, your knowledge will go far beyond fleeting insights. Instead, you'll actually change your behavior.

The Game helps you become aware of all the excuses you invent for not being great and excellent. The Game offers an opportunity to hold up a mirror to yourself. It turns into a microcosm for viewing your entire life through a magnifying glass and discovering the secret flaws that have kept you from having and doing everything you want.

The Game moves you out of a world where you complain about your problems, to one that rewards you for finding your greatest power under the most difficult circumstances. I'll show you the structure of The Game, but you'll be the one who goes through a process of discovery to learn what it's all about. You'll be setting your own goals for The Game—things you've wanted to accomplish for years. The Game will bring you out of habitual daydreaming, where your life is passing you by, into a joyful and playful expansion of your capacity to produce powerful results.

What Can Playing The Game Do for You Now?

In only three months, people who have played The Game have enthusiastically handled mounds of unfinished business—from cleaning out messy closets and garages to renewing and revitalizing unfulfilling relationships. Many individuals have taught themselves how to earn more money—even doubling their income while working less. Most Game-players have become healthier, feeling as if they have more vibrancy and energy.

Outstanding Game-players have stretched beyond self-interests into making life better and more satisfying for themselves and others. For example, George Thompson, a financial planner and stockbroker, designed a course to teach children how to manage money and play the stock market.

During her 90 days of playing The Game, one woman returned to Vietnam, her country of birth, and made appointments with Communist officials to enlist their support in educating Vietnamese girls and women—something the government has always considered unnecessary.

Andy Heath, an investment advisor, offered to donate half of his liver to a friend who needed a transplant. The list goes on and on with people who have played The Game and realized that they could make a difference in their own lives and the lives of others.

People who have played The Game with extraordinary

results were once like you. They wondered if their lives had meaning. They wanted life to be about more than paying off mortgages and hoping their future would be better than the present.

What if you were able to look back a decade from now to the time when you held this book in your hand for the first time and knew that you could make something powerful start to happen for you?

Please stop reading right now, and write today's date in your journal or on your calendar. Next to the date, write: "This is the day I started reading *The Game*."

Starting today, your life will become much more satisfying.

Why Play The Game?

Human beings are born with two fundamental questions that they spend their lives trying to answer. Those questions are: *Am I special?* and *Will I make a difference?*

I can answer the first one for you right now.

Yes, you are special. You're a snowflake with your own individual beauty and self-expression. Your uniqueness makes your life important to the world. You are not only special; you're irreplaceable.

Now for the second question: *Will you make a difference?*

Maybe.

Maybe, if you're clear about your higher purpose on this planet. Maybe, if you read this book and play The Game.

Maybe . . . but I can't be certain.

Many people, such as Gandhi, Martin Luther King, Jr., or Mother Teresa, have made an incredible difference in this world. Will you? This is a question you can answer by playing The Game. The Game gives you the opportunity to put your own house in order so you can look outside yourself and decide what meaning you want your life to have.

How Is The Game Played?

After reading this book, you'll play The Game by enlisting the aid of a partner. As a team, you'll register to play in The Game contest at **TheGameInteractive.com,** or mail the registration form in this book (on page 282) to us. During The Game, I suggest that you keep a Game journal of your experiences and use it for doing the exercises I've provided for you. In 90 days, you and your partner can refer back to your Game journal notes and write essays about your experiences. E-mail the essays to me at **TheGameInteractive.com** Website. Describe how playing The Game has transformed your life. Twice each year, we'll post essays we choose to be finalists, and you'll help me select The Game's winners. I'm offering a grand prize of $50,000 to the team that wins The Game. Eight other Game-players along with the grand prize winners will receive scholarships currently worth $18,000 per person. They'll have the opportunity to attend my company, **TheCoachingProgram.com's,** elite 15-month program where people who are committed to being their best receive intensive training.

I've specifically designed The Game so that you have the option of registering for it over the Internet or by mail; however, you can only *play* The Game over the Internet. By repeatedly returning to **TheGameInteractive.com** Website, you'll receive instructions from me, from skilled coaches, and from other Game players on how to achieve optimum results. In addition to showing you the value of getting help, I believe it's important to steer you toward the Internet because it's the wave of the future. I'm going to do whatever I can to encourage you to gain access to a worldwide body of knowledge. If you don't have a computer or Internet access, go to any public library and ask the reference librarian to show you how to log on and join the 21st century.

In The Game, you're competing to see who can lead the most extraordinary life in 90 days. By writing your essay for The Game contest, you'll start to recognize all the energy you've been investing in excuses and delays. The results you produce and the insights you gain will be a testament to why you played The Game in the first place. Your Game results will show what kind of player (in life) you'll be from now on.

As we journey through this book, you'll be reading about experiences from other Game-players. This will give you a glimpse of what is possible, even though you'll be creating your own path and deciding what goals are relevant to you.

One thing that's important to me (and should be to all of us) is raising the bar in The Game of Life by helping more people become players. The better everyone plays, the greater skills each of us will have to develop, and the more potential we'll tap. Let's face it—people in our highly technological world can't get into The Game unless they can read. That's why in addition to individual prizes, I'm focusing on eradicating adult illiteracy in America as one of my personal Game goals. I'll be beating the drum at every opportunity to support the work of literacy organizations throughout this country.

Ground Rules for The Game

The Game deepens your consciousness about the beauty of everyday existence and gives you access to creating new habits of your own choosing. Later in this book, I'll introduce more of the basic rules for The Game, but I want you to know five very important ones, so you can start to apply them right away.

1. One of the primary rules is that *you MUST give up self-criticism for 90 days.* You'll soon find that a lot of your positive actions were thwarted early on, before they became full-blown, as a result of always editing and criticizing yourself.

2. A second rule is to *be observant about what you're learning from playing The Game.* The Game is a journey, and this book is a conversation, with dialogue between us occurring inside your mind.

3. A third rule is that you *must stop whining and complaining for 90 days.* This means that while you play The Game, you'll make a conscious effort not to blame anyone else for how your life is going. Instead, with every challenge or problem, you won't waste time and energy moaning, but will immediately start taking responsibility for whatever is occurring.

4. The fourth rule is to remember that *The Game is a shared journey and a process of discovery.* This rule stems from a combination of the following principles that I'm asking you to remember as you read this book:

    *   *Even though I (Sarano Kelley) am the author, I'm never right.*
    *   *I don't know THE truth. This is an inquiry, a discovery process.*
    *   *I don't know more about anything than you do.*

5. The fifth basic rule for playing The Game is simple: *HAVE FUN!* Games are meant to be fun. This one is no exception.

What It's Like to Play The Game

Right now, release the goal of playing The Game perfectly. As soon as you try to inject the element of perfection, you'll come to a standstill. How many times in your life have you sacrificed *good* for *perfect?* You won't always live your life with the intensity of The Game. It wouldn't be balanced or healthy to do that. After you've played The Game for 90 days, you can rest and regroup between Games. Let new behaviors and habits settle in. Play again when you want to jump-start your life in another direction. This is a 90-day sprint.

Read this book all the way through before playing The Game. Afterwards, if you haven't completed all the exercises, return to each chapter and do them. At that point, it's time for you and your partner to register for your 90-day game. Approximately three months after starting The Game, you will have done one of two things: Either you will have produced powerful results, or you'll have a great explanation that makes perfectly good sense *to you* why you didn't win your life in 90 days.

In his speech before the 1996 Democratic National Convention, actor, director, and quadriplegic Christopher Reeve said:

> *"At first, something seems impossible. Then, it becomes improbable. But with enough conviction and support, it finally becomes inevitable."*

Do you want to seize the opportunity to win the life you've always wanted?

Join me on this journey. Let's play The Game—to win!

✳ ✳ ✳

PART I

What Does
The Game Promise?

*"I will never be the same. I have destroyed
my prior comfort zone. The Game has
become My Game. My Game has become
My Life. The Game is, in reality, a lifetime
journey. It has added structure and
accountability—two traits I passionately
resisted. It has added balance. My Game
has become an elaborate tool to guide
and monitor daily activities. It has become
my conscience to evaluate my life, to
continually adjust, fine-tune, rebalance,
and change the rules."*

— George Page, Player of The Game

✦ CHAPTER 1 ✦

Time

The Game promises to change your relationship with time by making it possible for you to do what's really important to you. By playing The Game, you'll learn to manage and prioritize time in ways that will allow you to enjoy a longer and more fulfilling life. You'll use time wisely to accomplish meaningful goals—even ones you've told yourself are impossible, given your busy schedule.

Humans invented the measurement of hours fairly early on in our history. Then we added minutes and seconds. We've only recently conceived of the nanosecond. We've forgotten that time is fiction, a simple measuring device we created in our history as a human race. We imbue time with significance, judge it as being "quality" or not, and race against it.

In **TheCoachingProgram.com's** classes, we ask: *Where are you rushing to?* You really have only one clear destination—six feet under the ground. Why would you be in such a hurry to get there? Why are you moving so fast that you can't stop to see the enormity, beauty, and wonder of the world in front of you? Why must you always put off your life until later, someday, when you have time? Why is *now* never quite good enough?

Shifting Your Time Priorities

Timothy Bellars says that before he played The Game for 90 days, it had only been his wife who gave their daughter a bath or brushed their son's teeth. Tim had always been too busy working and rushing around to spend much time with his children.

He says:

I think that there are two types of parents. Unfortunately, one spouse seems to spend a lot more time with the children, while the other one does not. I was the one who did not.

I have a certain relationship now with my two- and four-year-old that I know I would not have had if I hadn't played The Game, which made me get very precise about how I was spending my time. I saw that all of my business items were getting finished, and all my family things weren't. It became clear to me where I was prioritizing. I had to ask myself why I wasn't spending time with my kids. The answer really shocked me: They weren't important to me.

The fact is that I do what I think is a priority. If you said to me, "I'll give you a million bucks if you're on the phone at 1:15 A.M.," I'd be there at midnight waiting for that phone call. Being with my children wasn't a priority. I seemed to think it was more important for me to work. Now, that's sick. That's insane.

I was ignoring and taking my family for granted because I could. But it wasn't in their best interests or mine. I asked myself what kind of person I wanted to be. This gave me perspective on my life. I'd been like a mouse in a wheel, going around and around, doing stuff all day long. Playing The Game gave me the opportunity to get in line with who I want to be.

To help you change how you relate to time, I've designed a very simple *A-B-C-D* system for rating the value and immediacy of the things you do every day.

A Activities are those like the ones Tim described above, such as lovingly preparing your children for bed. *A Activities* nourish you. They include physical exercise, prayer, meditation, writing in a journal, and listening intently to family and friends. In The Game, your motto for *A Activities* will be: *Just do them!*

B Activities are reactionary. This is when the doctor tells you that if you don't exercise, you're going to die, as opposed to the *A Activity* of exercising without the threat of imminent demise. *B Activities* can be found in the world of crisis. In The Game, your motto for *B Activities* will be: *Eliminate these by getting them handled now.*

C Activities are those things that are best done by someone else. Making your children's beds when they could be doing this for themselves, or handling papers that a clerical assistant could be filing are *C Activities*. If you're like me, you may be a bit of a control freak. When I want something done, I feel I have to do it myself. This means that I'm often doing things others could do better. In The Game, your motto for *C Activities* will be: *Delegate these.*

D Activities steal and drain your energy. Time you spend daydreaming, gossiping, and criticizing yourself and others are *D Activities*. They produce little and take away a lot. In The Game, your motto for D Activities will be: *Stop doing these!*

By using this simple *A-B-C-D* system for categorizing how you spend your time, you'll be able to analyze why you're not being as highly productive and efficient as you could be. Engaging in *B*, *C*, and *D Activities* prevents you from fulfilling your life goals.

Time-Wasting Relationships

You can also look at how you spend your time in terms of the people you have relationships with. I've classified relationships as *A, B, C,* or *D.* This isn't for making judgments about people, but only to help you gain clarity on how you relate to them. Very fine and upstanding people can have inefficient or even hurtful relationships that bring out the worst instead of the best in each other.

A Relationships restore and nourish you. An example of an *A Relationship* would be a personal coach; or depending on your religious tradition, your priest, rabbi, or spiritual advisor. Certain ways of relating to spouses, family members, and friends form *A Relationships* because in an uncritical, loving way, these people hold you to a higher standard. *A Relationships* expect you to fulfill the purpose of your life, and this makes them priority relationships. You're engaging in an *A Relationship* when you spend time with yourself. Your motto for The Game will be: *Spend most of your time with* A Relationships.

B Relationships tend to maintain the status quo. Most friends, clients, and even family members fall into the category of *B Relationships.* I give friends a bum rap in The Game, because a friend typically accepts all the excuses you offer for not being great, and they may even supply some you haven't thought of. Friends often relate to your insecurities, because your fears and weaknesses are compatible with theirs.

B Relationships are often very nice and loving. In marriages, partners often become *B Relationships* for each other. You can transform a *B Relationship* into an *A Relationship* by asking the person to support you in achieving your goals, and to lovingly let you know when you're not keeping commitments to yourself. Your motto for The Game will be: *Transform* B Relationships *into* A Relationships.

C Relationships are the passersby in your life. They're

associates, and usually you can barely remember their names. They're not your friends. They're not contributing to your well-being and may be a drain on your time, energy, and other resources. Your motto for The Game will be: *Spend as little time as possible with* C Relationships.

*D Relationship*s are the people with whom you gossip, commiserate, or whine. D Relationships hurt you and take energy away from you. Your motto for The Game will be: *Spend no time at all with* D Relationships.

Before playing The Game, you'll want to analyze how much time you spend in *A Activities* with *A Relationships*. Let's say you're spending time with yourself. This, of course, is an *A Relationship.* But what if you're daydreaming the entire time you're alone? That would mean that you're not doing an *A Activity* with an *A Relationship.* Spending time alone and planning your day so it's more productive and fulfilling is an example of doing an *A Activity* with an *A Relationship.*

Here's a new rule for The Game:
Spend the majority of your day doing
A Activities *with* A Relationships.

Perhaps Game-player Greg Kadet summed up this principle best by saying, "Everything I do, every person I interact with, must further my destiny."

How Effective Are You?

I've noticed that most of us aren't willing to admit it, but we actually only work about 45 minutes to two hours a day. If you can't see it in yourself, maybe you have time-wasters in your office. They're the walking dead. This is why I say that most people are overwhelmed but underworked. The Game moves you toward becoming *under*whelmed and overworked.

Bill Meyer reports that after he'd been playing The Game for a while, one day his daughter said, "Dad, I used to like it when you puttered—you know, when you did things slowly and didn't ever finish them. It was cute. What is it that you're doing now—when you're working fast and getting things done?"

How much of your day, of your life, are you puttering away, spinning in circles without ever accomplishing much? To get yourself into motion right away, I suggest that you double your pace. You've probably been under the illusion all your life that only slow and steady wins the race. You've been told that moving quickly will cause you to make more mistakes. Sometimes this is true, but experiment. See if moving at double your usual pace really makes you less efficient. You may be surprised to find that for the most part, you haven't been working; you've been daydreaming.

What is the single most inefficient thing you do all day? Your most unproductive activity might be getting up and down for a cup of coffee or a cigarette. This most inefficient activity is something you'd classify for The Game as a *D Activity,* and you'll want to find a way to eliminate it so you can clear a space for more *A Activities.*

What's Important to You?

If you're ever going to change your relationship with time, you have to figure out what's important to you, as Tim Bellars did with his children.

Game-player Leslie Nelson says that by the age of 30, she'd spent most of her time pushing herself too hard at the expense of her personal life. After playing The Game for two weeks, Leslie suffered a lower back injury. This turned out to be something that showed her just how out of touch with her own needs she'd become. Leslie says that for two weeks, she was only able to work one hour a day, compared to her usual eight to ten hours.

She writes:

It took a couple of days for me to adjust to my physical limitations. I literally had to lie on the floor, because this was the only position that didn't cause severe pain.

To my surprise, I started getting used to and even enjoying being on the floor. I noticed the trees swaying in the breeze outside my window. I watched the fish swimming in the aquarium. I observed what goes on in my house during the day as the animals walked around. I'd missed all these things while I'd been so preoccupied, even though I worked at home.

During those precious two weeks of only working one hour and spending the rest of my time on the floor, I realized that I'd lost the joy of being present in my own life. I'd been so busy thinking about work that I'd removed myself from the things that were most important to me.

One morning after I'd had this profound realization, I woke up to find my 11-year-old dog sleeping next to me on my bed. She always used to sleep with me, and we had enjoyed doing everything together when she was a puppy. But I'd become a very busy person, and she'd started sleeping in the kitchen. Now, after a week of this back injury, when I'd returned to enjoying each moment and experiencing a return of my love for life, here she was, once again sleeping by my side on the bed. It was as if she was welcoming me back home. My dog's change in behavior had a huge impact on me emotionally. I now use her as a barometer for how present I am each day. I'm reminded by her nearness to meditate, relax, and keep my perspective.

All of this happened because I made a commitment to play The Game, which caused me to take a long, hard look at how I was spending my time. I discovered that I'd lost life's precious moments with my constant flurry of activity. I realized I'd been on a track that would have led to losing my good health. I was the kind of person who would have

had a heart attack in her 40s. I love to work. I never stop.
But constant work isn't good for my health.

During The Game, I completely re-created my schedule
to regain balance and perspective in my life.

Expanding Time with Multitasking

As you continue to play The Game and develop a wonderful partnership with your mind, you'll think of creative ways to accomplish more than one thing at a time. This is true multitasking, in which you maintain maximum focus, energy, and presence, while doing simultaneous noncompeting activities. Multitasking done well allows you to squeeze between the spaces of life and create more time for yourself.

Multitasking can teach you the difference between velocity and speed. I'm sure you've seen people who are working very fast with much exertion, effort, and a look of disgust or worry on their faces. They're focused on getting things finished quickly, and they're usually making a lot of mistakes. When speedy people try to multitask, others see them as being confused, busy, or overly ambitious.

Velocity is a different process. It's more like the experience of being "in the zone" or fully connected with what you're doing, as opposed to rushing or hurrying. When you're operating with velocity, you feel a sense of inner calm and peacefulness, as if you're outside of yourself watching what you're doing. With velocity, others see you accomplishing many things effortlessly while remaining focused and serene.

While playing The Game, you'll gain velocity by alternately focusing on working with velocity and quieting the mind and body by engaging in such practices as meditation, reflection, prayer, silence, or "Refreshing"—a practice I'll explain more completely later in this book.

Multitasking Versus Confusion

Sometimes people think they're multitasking, but they're just confused. They're driving, drinking coffee, and listening to the radio while trying to read the newspaper. I'd call that being distracted, not multitasking.

Examples of confusion are:

- *Eating while working.* These two tasks aren't compatible because working distracts you from fully tasting, chewing, and digesting your food.

- *E-mailing or typing while you're talking on the telephone.* These two activities are incompatible because you may respond with a lack of concentration to the e-mail, while giving the person on the other end of the phone the impression that you aren't fully listening.

- *Paying your bills while your children are trying to tell you something.* These activities are incompatible because your kids may feel that you're not interested in what they're saying or could think your frustration about your bills is being directed at them.

Examples of true multitasking, where you maintain focus and balance while doing simultaneous, compatible activities, are:

- *Reading a novel while pedaling a stationary bicycle.* These are compatible because the exercise is repetitive and doesn't require a lot of attention, and you can enjoy the act of reading as well.

- *Doing push-ups against the wall while riding in an elevator.* These are compatible activities because it's not necessary to be focused on anything while you're standing in the elevator, and pushing away from the wall doesn't require a lot of attention. Almost any kind of physical activity is compatible with waiting around for something to happen.

- *Listening to audiocassettes while driving in your car, or while running or walking.* This is a good use of time, since while driving or exercising, you might otherwise occupy your mind with meaningless daydreaming.

Multitasking by Collapsing and Folding Time

I've already shared my childhood fascination with comic books. Some other reading material that captured my attention as a child was science fiction, especially the classic series *Dune* by Frank Herbert. Some of the characters he wrote about had extraordinary powers. They could collapse space and fold time, which enabled them to travel across galaxies in an instant.

In The Game, you will learn how to be a time traveler, too—to collapse time and fold space. This means learning to bind together seemingly disparate activities that you want to accomplish—doing laundry while listening to classical music or an audio book—so they occur seamlessly and simultaneously. This is what you're doing while playing The Game—you're creating a seamless life where you can combine activities and gain the power of velocity.

On the other hand, your Game might require that you go in the opposite direction of multitasking in order to achieve a balanced life. Game-player Bill Meyer summarizes this idea effectively.

He says:

> *Time-packing, multitasking, and efficiency in all things are admirable skills to develop. But sometimes I just need to walk on the treadmill with no reading, no technology, and no company research, and be complete with doing one activity well. When I focus on one thing at a time like this, I take pleasure in the footfalls and the breathing. Sometimes a walk is just a walk.*

You decide how you want to change your relationship with time. After all, it's always *your* Game and *your* life.

Do I Have Time to Play The Game?

This is a question everyone asks, and Game-player Betty Lamb answers it beautifully. In her end-of-Game essay, Betty wrote about the 90 days she spent taking action instead of obsessing over how busy she was.

She writes:

> *How can a busy person like me ever find time to play The Game?*
>
> *My workout went from 70 to 90 minutes, and I started stretching before exercising as part of my normal routine. I find myself leaving places better than I found them. I make eye contact with as many people as possible. I do something nice for someone else each day. I thank my clients for their business before I end a phone call or meeting. I've learned how to operate my cell phone. I now own a personal laptop computer and a color printer.*
>
> *But I'm way too busy to focus on this goofy Game.*

EXERCISE: HOW MUCH IS MY TIME WORTH?

Write down what you want your annual income to be. Divide this amount by 52 to figure out your weekly rate. Then divide your weekly rate by 40 to get your hourly rate. Let's say, with these calculations, that you realize that to make the amount of income you desire, you should be earning $100 per hour. When you look at how you're spending your time each day, which activities are $100-per-hour tasks? Is watching television a $100-per-hour activity? Is finding out the birthdays of your best customers and sending cards to them worth $100? Is organizing your workspace for maximum productivity and efficiency a $100-per-hour task? Only you can decide. Based on what your hourly rate needs to be, decide if your typical daily activities are ones you should be doing, delegating, or eliminating.

EXERCISE: HOW ARE YOU SPENDING YOUR TIME?

Set up pages in your journal to look like the diagram below. For one or more days, keep a 15-minute log of your entire day's activities using the *A-B-C-D* rating system I introduced earlier. This is your base use of time. Do this log again at the end of your 90-day Game so you can compare how you've changed your priorities and your relationship with time.

Time	Activity	Activity A-B-C-D Rating	With Whom?	Relationship Rating
6:00	Hit the snooze alarm	*D Activity*	Self	*A Relationship*
6:15	Make coffee	*C Activity*	Husband	*B Relationship*

As you analyze your day, notice the following:

- Which *D Activities* can you eliminate?
- Which *B Activities* could become *A Activities*, such as getting a physical instead of waiting to find out that you're ill?
- Which C Activities could you delegate?
- Which *A Activities* could be expanded or combined?
- When are you using your time most efficiently?

Also, look at how much time you're spending with *B, C,* and *D Relationships.* Could this time be spent more productively?

Refer to your hourly rate above, and decide which activities and relationships aren't worth your time . . . based on how much your time is worth.

Exercise: Planning Your Powerful Day

Plan a powerful day by spending the major portion of your time doing *A Activities* with *A Relationships* at your peak efficiency times. Start by figuring out how you'll do more nourishing things for yourself, your family, and the people you love. Then see how much time is left for work. By eliminating as many *B, C,* and *D Activities;* and *B, C,* and *D Relationships* as possible, notice how much of your day opens to more productive and satisfying habits, practices, and relationships.

Next, look at your powerful day to analyze when you might multitask or expand time and fold space. How could you combine activities and relationships, or move at double your usual pace? Could you get up earlier to experiment with morning efficiency, thereby making more time for yourself?

* * *

In this chapter, you've been given some powerful tools and concepts for changing your relationship with time while you play The Game. Now you're going to move more deeply into The Game by learning about the first of three major building blocks for winning your life.

* * *

Chapter 2

Structure

T he Game promises to help you find practical yet creative
ways for structuring your life in order to achieve your goals.
Think about some of the things you've always wanted to
do. They could be as simple as remembering to floss your teeth
or as complex as mastering a foreign language. Wouldn't it be
great if you could design systems to help you have or eliminate anything? Well, now you can.

One aspect of life that has made things more difficult for
people today is our fundamental loss of *structure*. Many of the
traditional foundations—marriage, family, and church—gave
our society efficiency and cohesiveness, and people used to rely
on the structure of corporations for their long-term care and
income. Now, many of these structures have weakened or no
longer exist.

Structure Works

In most cases, unless you put some type of structure in place
to make something happen for you, it simply won't happen. I'm
defining *structure* to mean everything outside of yourself that

makes it easier for you to do something. Structure helps you keep your word to yourself and others.

Game-player Tim Bellars feels strongly about the importance of keeping commitments to himself, but although he'd been trying to lose weight forever, he'd always given himself escape hatches. While playing The Game, Tim set up the structure of hiring a personal trainer and later switched to working out with a partner who is a competitive bodybuilder. These structures provided Tim with coaches who helped him use good form and technique while achieving maximum results and risking less injury.

Each day for 12 weeks, Tim used the structure of keeping a log of his workouts, what he ate, and how he felt after eating. Writing down exactly what he was doing and eating helped Tim see his progress and discover when he was sabotaging himself.

Tim also found that setting up the structure of a predictable exercise routine helped him save time. He says that he'd wake up, put on clothes that he'd set out the night before, drink one glass of water, eat his first of seven small meals for the day, and drive to the gym. This was a structure he didn't have to think about that turned into an art form of efficiency. Before he put this structure into place, it used to take him 30 minutes to get ready in the morning. The structure of routine and planning helped him get out of the house in only 15 minutes. When Tim arrived at the gym, he and his workout partner had previously decided what body parts they'd be concentrating on strengthening, what exercises they'd do, and how many repetitions and sets they'd perform. They wasted no time in indecisiveness.

Tim and his wife also attacked the structures of their refrigerator and pantry and tossed out a garbage can full of junk food. They agreed that for 90 days, they'd only allow food into their house that complied with their new diets. They even bought new cookbooks.

Tim says, "I started eating like I meant it. Before I'd eat anything, I'd ask myself, *Does this piece of food further emphasize who I say I am?* If I'm a physically fit guy, do I eat cheese puffs? Probably not."

So, what happened with all the structures Tim designed for himself? He's happy to announce that he lost 25 pounds during his 90-day Game. At long last, he'd kept his commitment to himself. By playing The Game wholeheartedly, designing structures caused Tim to be the accountable person he'd always wanted to be.

Examples of Structures

What's missing when you say, "I want to work out," but you're not doing it?

More than likely, working out isn't happening because you haven't scheduled it. Have you written a workout time and place on your calendar? You may be a person who schedules your entire day, but you fool yourself into thinking that you're going to squeeze a workout in somewhere, sometime. Your scheduled meetings and appointments are happening; the workout isn't. What's the difference?

Scheduling is a very simple structure. It keeps you from meandering and merely reacting to whatever is happening to and around you. So, take the time to plan your day so that the things you claim you want to do actually end up happening.

Clothes are one of life's best structures. If you're feeling fat, you're probably wearing clothes that don't fit. These clothes become a structure or a reminder of your negative self-image. One of the simple ways to improve your self-image is to wear clothes that fit. If you can't find good-fitting clothes, have them altered. This, by itself, totally changes the way you appear to others and to yourself. Structures end up reinforcing each other. If you want to be more athletic, your structure would be to buy yourself a workout suit you really like and are proud to be seen in. This creates an inducement for you to put it on and exercise.

Game-player George Thompson, who lost 30 pounds in his 90-day Game, offers yet another novel idea for creating a structure that gets results.

George says:

> *The biggest thing I did to make a structure for myself was to carry a stopwatch with me at all times. I'd use it to measure how long I was spending with tasks or in conversations. If someone came by to talk to me, they'd see my stopwatch and know I was serious. If you were in the gym and saw a guy running down the stairs with a log on his back, you wouldn't come up to him and start talking about nothing.*
>
> *Before playing The Game and adding the structure of carrying a stopwatch, I estimate that I was productive about 40 minutes each day. During The Game, I became truly productive about four hours a day. What's more, I could do in a day what used to take me a week to accomplish. I gained this kind of power by learning to control my own schedule instead of letting other people and interruptions regulate how I'd be spending my time.*

Structuring Your Social Life

I've had men and women come to me for coaching because they're tired of living their lives alone. They work long hours, but their personal lives are in a shambles. They rarely date, and can count on the fingers of one hand how many satisfying relationships they've ever had. Of course, for some of these people, it's necessary to find a therapist who can help them understand the deeper issues that might be causing this kind of isolation and loneliness. But I try to help them discover how they've been structuring their lives to avoid dating. Then we figure out what changes to make so they can start having a social life.

Sometimes, as we analyze their situation, I notice that my clients are very critical of every prospective date or love interest. They've set up a structure of rudeness and nitpicking to keep themselves at home alone. We also look at the structure of their hairstyle and clothing, which sends unconscious messages to prospective dates that they're unavailable. One woman, for example, always styled her hair so that it obscured her face.

In **TheCoachingProgram.com,** many of the most romantically challenged people have changed their mind-sets and have revised how they present themselves to the world. They've also altered the structure of their routines. Instead of going straight home after work, I've advised them to get involved in charities or to pursue interests and hobbies they've always been curious about. As a result of these changes in their structures, they've created more balance in their lives.

The Freedom of Structure

While playing The Game, structures will free you to devote your energy to engaging in the process fully and enthusiastically. Structure is an element that inspires you to get serious about The Game, yet it's also a key to having more fun. Gameplayer Stephen Masri says, "I achieved things I've always wanted to do by putting them into The Game, which became fun itself. As I found myself accomplishing things, I really began to enjoy the process."

Without structure, it's very easy to run in circles. In so many areas of your life, you're repeatedly dealing with the same issues. Structure allows you to stop sidestepping uncomfortable aspects of your life and helps you to better understand and resolve them.

After you've decided what you want to see happening in your life, get creative about how you can structure your day, your relationships, and your resources to win your life. Remember, structure makes your life happen.

EXERCISE: WHAT STRUCTURES DO I NEED?

List some activities you've always wanted to do. Next to each item on your list, design structures for putting these things into motion. For example, maybe you've been trying to organize your messy garage or closets but have only succeeded in whining about never having time to do these onerous tasks. Before you start cleaning, call a local charity and arrange for the time and date that a pickup truck will arrive to haul off all your donations, or put an ad in the paper announcing a yard sale. Observe how the structure of having a deadline moves you into action and keeps your momentum going.

EXERCISE: OBSOLETE STRUCTURES

With this exercise, you're going to analyze structures that are keeping your bad habits and negative traits in place. List what you consider to be your worst habits and the most negative aspects of your personality. They can be things such as faultfinding, wasting time or money, or not keeping your commitments. You know what they are. Now draw a chart for yourself like the diagram on the next page, and fill it in.

Negative Habit or Trait	Environment, Time, or Object Structures Keeping This in Place	People Structures Keeping This in Place
Being overly critical.	I gossip in the lounge while I'm drinking coffee.	Julie is my best gossip buddy during break time.
Eating high-calorie doughnuts in the morning.	I don't plan for eating breakfast, so I'm hungry before lunch.	My friends and I eat doughnuts every day during our breaks.
Feeling like I'm a victim.	I watch and listen to low-quality news shows that make me feel upset about what's going on in the world.	Jerry and I talk about the news, and I start to feel upset about all the bad things that can happen to people.

Next, decide what actions you could take to change the environment, objects, times, and ways you relate to people so it's easier to put an end to your negative habits and traits.

✳ ✳ ✳

Now I'm going to show you how to become successful in The Game by associating with people who love to do those things that you don't.

★ CHAPTER 3 ★

Affinity

The Game promises that you can learn to love and even be proficient at skills and habits that you never thought you'd excel at. Have you ever noticed how easy it is for you to perform tasks or activities when you feel love, passion, enjoyment, or attraction for them? I call this process *affinity*, and it's one of the fundamental prerequisites for playing The Game successfully.

If you're an avid golfer, you don't need to put "Play golf today" on your To-Do list. At the same time, there might be aspects of golf that you have to remind yourself to practice because you're not confident with them, so they're not enjoyable. Or you might delay buying a new pair of golf shoes because you don't have an affinity for shopping. Affinity shows up as love. When you're doing something you love, you have an affinity for it.

Now, look at many of the things you've wanted to do or have happen in your life but which aren't occurring. I'm going to show you how to develop an affinity for them.

You're Not Going to Love Everything

Let's face it—you're not going to develop an affinity for everything you want to do in life. Some things will probably never come easily or naturally for you, or it may take a long time for an affinity to develop. When you don't have an affinity for something, especially a skill or goal you would like to have in your Game, it's crucial to find someone to partner with who loves what you're trying to learn. You need to associate with people who support and model what you want to have happen in your life.

Let's say you don't like working out, but you've decided to increase physical exercise during your 90-day Game. This doesn't mean you're going to suddenly love going to the gym or running around the track every day. But do you know someone who *does* have a passion for working out?

Arielle Ford, who is a Game-player, my agent, and the publicist for this book, says, "When I played The Game for my health, I hired a personal trainer and paid him in advance to coach me. This meant that he was waiting at the gym for me. If I didn't show up, I'd wasted his time and my money." Arielle's approach is to find people who have an affinity for whatever you want to develop. It's fine to associate with people who love what they do, but if you pay them to teach you, you're more likely to stay motivated to learn from them.

Every athlete has a coach. When you play The Game, you'll have a partner, and the two of you will coach each other through the 90 days. Perhaps you wonder why you need a partner or coach. Well, how has it worked for you to try to do everything by yourself? Where has total independence and self-reliance gotten you? Have you accomplished all you wanted and all you're capable of? Have you fulfilled your purpose in life?

A consistent characteristic of those who have become great is that they love what they do. Love drives them forward. This is what I mean by affinity. People who have a strong affinity for what they do are those you want to associate with and get to know well.

I had the opportunity early in my career on Wall Street to work for one of the wealthiest investment bankers in the world. This was a gentleman with a net worth in excess of a half-billion dollars. After working at his firm, I became a broker in the office of one of the world's most successful securities salesmen, Martin Shafirof. He'd been written about in a book that lauded the ten greatest salespeople in the world. During the time I worked in his office, Marty was said to have produced $20 million in commissions in a single year. Watching him in action completely fascinated me. It also raised the question in my mind: *Why do some people produce extraordinary results, while others fail?*

I'd found myself on both ends of this success-failure equation and wondered what it would take to be consistently and predictably excellent. I knew that there were moments when I was excellent. The problem was that those moments seemed arbitrary. After I learned and began to apply the technology of The Game, which included using affinity to help me attain my goals, I was able to achieve excellence in all areas of my life.

How Affinity Helps You Meet Your Goals

Let's say you want to be a really good husband or wife. One of the first things you'd do is seek out those individuals who are already great spouses, those who really love performing that role well. Then you'd spend time observing and interacting with these super-spouses. By doing so, you'd be watching and imitating those who are better than you are at something and who have fun doing it.

You might also go to marriage counseling or read articles and books on how to be a more attentive husband or wife. Despite the effort it takes to develop your relationship skills, you'd develop an affinity for improving the relationship with your own spouse. You'd find that you really love relationship work, when the result is a happier and more fulfilling family life.

Affinity can also lead to structure. When you tell people who constantly work at making their marriages more exciting and fulfilling that this is something *you're* trying to do, they're likely to say, "Oh, you should get this book or subscribe to this magazine. It gives great advice and practical examples." Then you have a structure, because you're reading about more people who have an affinity for marriage. These basic elements of The Game—structure and affinity—work together to get you started and continue your momentum.

Reverse Affinity

Affinity relationships can hold you accountable to your goals through a kind of reverse affinity called *friendly competition*. Game-player George Thompson says:

> *I used to say to myself, "I'm going to lift weights tomorrow." But I needed only the slightest excuse not to work out. During The Game, I was lifting weights because I knew it was part of my Game and I wanted to beat Greg Kadet. We have this rivalry thing going. When I thought about skipping my workout, I'd say to myself, "I bet Greg is in the gym right now lifting weights." Then I'd call him and we'd compare notes about who had lifted the heaviest weights or done the most repetitions. The fun of competition made both of us work harder.*

Another example of affinity in reverse happens with students and their study habits. How many kids study with a friend who is even more distracted and worse at studying than they are? To improve study habits, the first thing you'd do is create a structure such as going to a library, a quiet place that is conducive to studying. Then you'd choose the people to study with who love whatever it is you're trying to learn, whether it's geometry or biology. Why would you study biology with someone who has less of an affinity for it than you do? Yet students do this kind of reverse affinity all the time and wonder why their grades don't improve.

While on the subject of education in school, I want to point out what I think is a downfall of our current American system. It's structured in a way that fundamentally doesn't work because the system destroys affinity. The people who are responsible for raising and teaching our children are paid the least, while athletes and movie stars are paid the most. It's an interesting way to spend our money as a culture. We're forcing out many teachers who have an affinity for their subject because they're burnt out and underpaid. Since they love their subject, they'll be tempted to go where they can excel at it *and* earn a higher income. This creates a loss of affinity in education.

Affinity Can Change Your Life

When I look back at my life, I see how my affinity or love for a subject was usually sparked by one special teacher. There always seemed to be one person who so loved a particular subject that I couldn't help but get caught up in what they were teaching.

I remember really hating math and finding it extremely difficult. Even though I studied economics in college and became a stockbroker, I hated the mathematics part of my work. Then one day, when I was helping to run the training department of Kidder Peabody, I met Stu Veale. He looked a lot like a youthful version of Santa Claus. We hired him to teach bond math. Since by then I was the teacher and not the student, I had the option of ducking out of his classes. But I started hearing so many great things about Stu that I figured I'd sit in just to get acquainted with his teaching style. Several hours into class, I found myself with a calculator in my hand, feeling overjoyed at discovering how the mathematical concepts of convexity and duration related to bonds. If you'd told me that I would have had any chance of getting turned on to mathematics in Stu's class, I'd have said there was a better chance that I'd eat a tree-bark sandwich for lunch.

I'd forgotten the impact a master of any subject can have on even the most closed-minded student. What captured my interest was Stu's glee, his humor, and his sheer joy at being able to take us from a state of ignorance to one of confidence. From that experience, I began to doubt all of my long-held beliefs about what I didn't like and what I couldn't do.

Life's Unlikely Teachers

When you seek out people who have an affinity for a skill, interest, or discipline, you may be surprised to find that the individuals you choose to align yourself with aren't friends, or even people you like. Sometimes friends hold you in patterns that aren't in the best interests of developing affinity. They support your bad habits instead of helping you develop more fulfilling ones.

In my own life, as I sought to mold myself into a greater human being, I found myself no longer seeking out the company of negative, complaining, or reactive people. I didn't reject them as people; I merely stopped creating circumstances that put me in the company of those who thought it was a badge of honor to exhibit contempt for just about everything. The power of affinity is that you lose your taste for the mean, the petty, and the small.

Affinity Doesn't Equal Warm and Fuzzy

Affinity doesn't mean you only associate with people you like or who make you feel good. The interesting thing about life is that we often shy away from the very people who can help us most.

After I entered the business world, I realized that I needed to seek out the best teachers and, if need be, work under them for free. My list of mentors has included one of the wealthiest people in the world, who taught me the entrepreneurial spirit and showed me that people can raise themselves up from nothing. The former CEO of the Saatchi and Saatchi advertising agency brutally yet lovingly coached me on attention, discipline, and the value of having a spiritual focus in any and all activities. Yet he also showed me that affinity isn't necessarily warm, fuzzy, or nice, because what you're going for is excellence. To become excellent, you may need to spend time with people who annoy you or even hurt your feelings.

Linda Anderson, who has helped me write this book, tells the story of developing an affinity for playwriting from a very gruff master of the craft.

She says:

> I'd go home in tears after turning scenes in to my play-writing teacher that I'd so carefully written. He'd throw my work back across the desk, and in his deep, authoritative voice, say, "Dig deeper." I'd go home, crying and whining to my husband, saying, "He doesn't like anything I write. He's so tough on me." But this man loved theater and good plays. He refused to accept anything but my very best. To please him or to show him—I don't know which it was, probably a combination of both—I wound up writing plays under his direction that won three national awards. I had another teacher at the theater who gave me lots of encouragement, and I loved her. She helped bolster my self-confidence with

her affinity for theater, too. But the "dig deeper" man really spurred me to work harder at my craft even though he scared the living daylights out of me.

Using Affinity to Win Your Life

You can develop affinity by doing difficult things until you develop a natural love for them. Believe it or not, if you pay enough attention to anything, you'll learn to love it. You don't love things when you're not present to them, and fear or anxiety is destroying your focus. When you do something for the first time, it's probably going to be difficult unless you're a natural at it. With practice and attention, you gain efficiency, beauty, and love.

You may have spent many painful hours practicing scales while learning to play the piano, and feel you have no affinity for this skill. But when people gather around you at parties to sing their favorite songs, you enjoy being the life of the party. From that point on, you have an affinity for practicing piano and learning new pieces, because now you do it well and have reaped the benefits of persistence.

Let Children Teach You Affinity

Children seem to have an affinity for everything. My daughter, Georgia, loves to play games, and she's a voracious and enthusiastic player. She always begins The Game immediately and doesn't forget her goals. Once in action, she stays in action. When we play The Game with each other, I find myself lagging behind, going in fits and starts, but she plays on a more even basis and often beats me.

Finally, I saw my chance to find something I could play Georgia for in our Games and win. One day, she told me that she'd been having persistent stomachaches for several months. Her mother and I examined her diet and noticed that she was eating very concentrated foods—chicken, French fries, pizza, pasta—and drinking little or no water. I'd been hearing that, since our bodies are mostly composed of water, people need to drink as much as a gallon a day. Certainly we need at least the eight glasses most health professionals recommend. So I suggested that Georgia's problem might be dehydration. I confessed that I, too, rarely drank as much water as I should.

Well, my daughter immediately saw possibilities for adding the objective of drinking more water as a goal in the fun Game structure of competing, scoring, and giving ourselves points. We decided that the prize for drinking the most water during a week would be that the person who drank the least would wait on the other one hand and foot.

This was exactly what I'd hoped for. I knew I could win the Water Game. I really looked forward to watching Georgia clean out my closet and fold my laundry for a day.

We'd no sooner struck our deal when I saw Georgia walk out of the living room, go to the kitchen, and pour herself a glass of water. I thought, *What a little cheater. She's starting off immediately. If I'm going to win, I have to get moving right away, too.*

After playing the Water Game with Georgia for a week, I discovered that I was becoming thirstier. Before this, I could go an entire day only drinking two cups of coffee and two glasses of orange juice. I hardly ever drank water, yet I felt fine. When I started drinking a gallon or two of water each day, my body developed an affinity—a love for water. If I went a day without drinking at least one gallon, I could tell the difference. It's amazing how quickly things can shift—even in your body—when you have an affinity for them.

While playing the Water Game, I learned that one of the great benefits of developing an affinity for something is losing your self-consciousness about developing new habits. By making drinking more water part of The Game I played with Georgia, I became so determined to win that I started carrying a gallon jug of water to fancy-schmancy restaurants where I had business meetings. I didn't feel at all self-conscious about this bizarre behavior. All I wanted to do was beat Georgia at The Game. It didn't matter what anyone else thought.

Georgia carried a jug of water with her everywhere, too, while we played the Water Game. And by now, you can probably guess the outcome of this story. By the end of our week of playing the Water Game, Georgia had solidly trounced me. It's lots of fun, but very difficult, to compete with someone who has such an affinity for playing The Game. Georgia is an inspiration to me because she understands so well that life can only happen by taking action *now,* rather than merely *thinking about* what you want to do.

EXERCISE: WHO LOVES TO DO THIS?

List three goals you're already aware of that you want to achieve in your 90-day Game. You can start with things you want to do but have failed at, are afraid to do, or dislike doing. Next to each goal, be specific about the skills, practices, and disciplines that you'll need to develop in order to achieve those goals.

Next to each of these skills, write the name of a specific person or type of individual you believe has an affinity for these habits and behaviors you want to develop.

✳ ✳ ✳

Goals	Skills, Practices, and Disciplines	Affinity People
Become a better parent.	Help Evan with his homework.	Apply lessons to activities Evan and I enjoy, such as using math for baseball stats.
	Join the PTA.	Go with my best friend, Gary, to the next PTA meeting.
Become a better husband.	Read books on romancing one's mate.	Ask George, who I think is a really great husband, how he shows Marilyn that he loves her.

＊ ＊ ＊

Now we're going to expand on the concepts of structure and affinity to include more people and resources . . . to help you win your life in ways you never thought possible.

＊ ＊ ＊

★ Chapter 4 ★

Community

The Game promises that when you reach out to other people and communicate with them about your aspirations, their resources and energy will bring you incredible support in fulfilling your purpose. While playing The Game, you're going to have the experience of hearing fans giving you standing ovations and cheering as you win your life.

Along with structure and affinity, *community* is the third basic element of The Game to support your quest of winning your life in 90 days.

This book creates a community out of anyone who plays The Game. When you go to **TheGameInteractive.com** Website, your community expands to the people who are interested in making a difference in themselves and the planet.

The principle of community flies in the face of our sense of individualism and self-sufficiency. Yet very few human beings are truly solitary creatures. Game-player Arielle Ford gives a great example of how structure, affinity, and community can help you achieve your Game goals.

Arielle writes:

I was certain that I could never be a "morning person," and that it was unrealistic to think I'd ever get out of bed before 8:00 A.M. After I committed myself to playing The Game, it became evident that for me to reach my fitness goals, I'd have to exercise in the early morning. So I bought an alarm clock [structure], *and I noticed that the strangest thing started to happen. Each morning, two minutes before the alarm went off, I'd wake up. Then I'd drag my lazy butt out of bed at 6:45 and walk four miles with my walking partner* [structure and affinity].

I made a wonderful discovery in this process. I found that I didn't need to be fully awake to walk. I just had to get myself out the door. The night before, I'd always lay out my clothes along with a nutrition bar, water, and sunglasses, so I could quickly, though sleepily, get into motion [structure]. *I noticed that my pattern was to become fully conscious about 30 minutes into my walk.*

People who know me were stunned. Even my neighbors seemed to admire the fact that I was actually out of bed and walking so early in the morning. It felt good to be the subject of that kind of neighborhood gossip [community].

Community Resources

I use the term *community* to represent the treasure chest of resources you have to draw upon in this world. Every person you interact with brings more skills, talents, knowledge, relationships, and perspective to your life. Whenever you add a person to your community, you've increased your available resources. Eliminating someone from your community potentially limits your resources.

When you create a powerful community, you fold space like

the heroes I used to read about in science fiction. Communities allow you to take resources that are farther away, and bring them closer to you. If your community extends to the world, somewhere on the globe there's someone who can help you accomplish your goals. Increasing your network increases your strength.

Loy Gotham shared an example of how she creatively found ways for her community to help with one of her major goals. She says:

One of my most significant breakthroughs while playing The Game has been in the area of physical fitness. I've always been an active person. I walk my dogs two or three miles most days, and I spend countless hours with a wheelbarrow and shovel, working in my garden. I also enjoy downhill skiing in the winter. But I haven't had a formal fitness program for almost four years. Because summers in Minnesota are so short, I prefer to spend my evenings outdoors rather than in a stinky gym. Since I normally work through my lunch hour, this leaves only mornings for working out. I am not a morning person. It's very difficult for me to make it to the gym at 6:00 A.M.

I begged my friends and co-workers to meet me at the gym. I knew I'd show up if I made a commitment to someone else, but I found it hard to keep the commitment to myself.

One day, my sister-in-law called me. Her family prays together every evening. She told me I was on their prayer list for the week. She wanted to know if there was anything I'd like them to pray for. I said that it would be a tremendous help if they prayed for me to have the strength to get up early and work out.

The same day my sister-in-law called, I talked to John, my partner in The Game. I made a commitment to him to get to the gym the very next morning.

The first few times I worked out in the morning before

going to my office, I was so excited that I came to work and told everyone. Every time I exercised in the morning, I called John and crowed that I'd made it to the gym again. I also reported the results to my sister-in-law and her family. I wanted them to know that their prayers had been answered right away.

Loy discovered the power of having a supportive community. Most of us experience a diminished community as we grow older, as we are no longer making friends and meeting people through school activities. What you may not have noticed is that reduction of community has also brought about a contraction of your resources.

Communities Make Things Happen

By now, you're probably starting to formulate some goals you'd like to achieve by playing The Game. Take a look at anything you've wanted to accomplish but haven't, and see if these are things you tend to do alone. Are you the only person in the game of your unrealized dreams? When you analyze the accomplishments in your life, do you notice that these are activities you did with other people? The nature of good company is that it elevates the mind and opens the heart.

Some people will say, "Oh, I should read more." Okay, great, so what about starting a reading club? Or "I should write more." Okay, great, so why not write with a partner? Why not take a writing class or go to a writer's conference where everybody is writing?

For many of us in the coaching program, a new community was created when we found out that one of our program participants was expected to die from a liver disease. A highly functional community formed around this man's struggle to stay alive. The coaching community rallied and helped the man consult health professionals he needed, offered him encouragement and prayers, and raised $25,000 so he could have the option of a liver transplant. Four people in this man's coaching class offered to donate half of their livers. One class member even underwent surgery for this purpose. Communities can become highly functional when they're aligned behind purposes higher than self-service and personal gain.

Dysfunctional Communities

Some communities support your being stuck in the past. One of the problems you may have encountered when trying to achieve results so far in your life is that you're in a community that believes that success is wrong or dishonest. This is an example of a dysfunctional community that impedes your progress and causes you to take a step backward for every move forward. Some communities band together to thwart you out of jealousy or the need to maintain the status quo.

A person could be very poor and be a part of a community that in its own way is committed to poverty. All of a sudden, one member excels. This success says, in effect, to the rest of the community, "I'm doing better. Why aren't you?" If the community were to support this person's act of breaking out of the pack, they'd have to take responsibility for where *they* are.

Perhaps in the course of playing The Game, you'll discover a clearer purpose for yourself other than making as much money as you can. People in your community might ask with disdain if you're taking some kind of self-improvement class. You may discover that you're part of a community that isn't supporting your new aims and desires.

Recognizing Dysfunctional Communities

How can you tell if your community is dysfunctional? Here's an example. I've met people in Alcoholics Anonymous (AA) who don't drink and are happy about it. They're a functional community. I've met other groups of people in bars who were having a really great conversation, were enjoying life, and were committed to being a positive force. They're also a functional community. Both of those communities are cohesive and supporting each other's goals even though they're engaged in different habits for different reasons.

An example of a dysfunctional community would be alcoholics who aren't clear about their commitment to sobriety, and who hang out with people who encourage or even ridicule them into drinking. Then, toss into this community some people who don't approve of or like to drink at all. That's what I would consider a dysfunctional community. No one is supporting anyone else in this kind of community.

Some communities worked for you in the past but may not meet your needs today. The communities you belong to may be perfect for someone else but not good for supporting *you*. This group of individuals may no longer inspire you, but if you found the *right* kind of community, you'd regain inspiration. This is an important point in reevaluating your communities. For The Game, you don't only need communities that are competent in their support of your goals; they must inspire you to achieve them and to live your higher purpose.

This principle also applies to your business or work community. You could say that you want a certain amount of income in your life and figure out your new financial goals for playing The Game. Then you go to work every day and think your work community will support your goal of having more money in your life. When you look at it more closely, you might realize that this community isn't supporting you at all. Maybe you're part of a sales staff with co-workers who undercut each other, or the people in your office don't support you sufficiently to make increasing your income possible. Instead, they detract from your goals.

In the consulting I've done, I have seen many businesses where the different communities within the organization worked against each other. Ultimately, the larger community of the business is incredibly dysfunctional, even though there might be some highly functional people in certain divisions of it. The loss of productivity is incalculable.

A community is often defined by whether it's *for* something or *against* something. Either type of community can be powerful. But the most powerful, effective, and functional communities are *for* something. Unfortunately, many of the most destructive communities arise from groups that are against something. It's almost as if they lack any reason for existence outside of their opposition to "outsiders."

Also, some communities are rigid, while others are structured. A community can maintain solid structure and still not be threatened by variety. This is the difference between a cult and a community. Cultish groups are rigid, and new members who don't fit in to their way of viewing the world are made to feel inferior or wrong. This type of community has been formed to exclude everyone else.

Look at the things you don't like in your life, and figure out which weaker, dysfunctional communities are supporting them. Ask yourself what you *do* and *do not* want in your life any longer. You may be surprised to note that certain communities are supporting habits and behaviors you now realize you don't want. It will become very clear which communities are functional or dysfunctional for you. Then it's up to *you* to join or form new ones, extricate yourself from obsolete ones, or inspire dysfunctional communities to help you keep the commitment to give your all for 90 days.

How Communities Have Helped and Hurt Me

As a young child, I didn't care a lot about having friends in my neighborhood. But when I reached my teens, the loneliness and isolation from my peers became unbearable. I felt the need to belong to a community. Where I lived in Brownsville, New York, this meant hanging out with a gang of street kids and being tough.

I was still a little more studious than most of the kids I hung out with, but I lost interest in my studies and stopped talking to my teachers. I began to isolate myself from my family by spending less time with them. As a member of this gang, it was considered uncool to be seen with anyone other than the tough kids, so I began to rob myself of all the communities that had previously supported and nurtured me.

One day, I was wearing this really nice watch my parents had bought for me. A kid who was tougher than I was mugged me and beat me up. I was totally humiliated. After this incident, the gang didn't mind that I wanted to leave it, because they'd always called me "The Brainiac" and considered me to be inferior. I finally figured out that belonging to this group wasn't authentic for me.

After leaving this dysfunctional community, I met two of my closest friends in life, Fred Scarboro and Kevin McNeil. They were more like me, athletic but primarily studious. These guys were very involved with their families, too. We formed our own community. It was because of my association with Fred and Kevin that I graduated from high school at the age of 16. In the community I formed with these new friends, it was cool to be a student teacher. So, not only did I do well in school, but I also taught younger kids. The unwritten code of my new community was generosity of spirit; meanness was never tolerated or encouraged.

If I had continued with the gang, I'd be in a different place today. This is what happens when you choose a community to meet your needs of the moment rather than supporting your-self in achieving your higher purpose.

Creating Highly Functional Communities

Our coaching-program clients notice that when they first start to play The Game and return to their work environments, they feel different from co-workers, family members, and friends who haven't made a commitment to personal and community excellence. Soon they come to understand that if they want functional communities in their lives, Game-players have to take responsibility for creating them.

Because his heart was opening and his love for life increased while playing The Game, Eric Bodner did a spontaneous act of kindness that brought his work community together. On Valentine's Day, he gave roses to every single woman in his office. Eric is a very powerful executive in a large corporation, yet for years, he'd walked through his office without really notic-ing or connecting with the people around him. The staff was totally blown away by his Valentine's Day gift. Many of them hadn't received anything from *anyone*, yet someone who was basically a stranger to them had given them flowers.

Following his gesture of appreciation, Eric noticed how much easier it was for him to get things done around the office. Although he hadn't expected anything in return as a result of giving this gift from his heart, Eric had created a new and sup-portive relationship within his work community.

While you're playing The Game, you, too, can create pow-erful communities to support you by following a basic rule of The Game. That rule is: *Invite everyone to support you, and push your Game on no one.* In The Game, you're not trying to impose a way of life on other people. The Game is between *you* and *you*. If, because of your example, people want to par-ticipate in certain aspects of The Game with you, that's great, but it's not required. As the Game-player, you have to learn not to go into a holier-than-thou attitude.

The attitude and behavior of leading by example instead of by coercion or domination is powerful. People will see what you're doing and like it or want it. One of the best ways to share what you're learning by playing The Game is by *doing* instead of talking.

As others see positive changes in your life, community will start to build around you. It might be one person, then five or ten who see a difference in you. Before you know it, like-minded people are supporting you and each other in their greatness.

The key to success is giving people the opportunity to support your Game by making it very clear that this is something *you're* up to with no expectations from them. I certainly don't recommend that you say to someone, "You know, there's a lot of stuff you could fix about yourself. Here's a book to read." No one would find that approach very endearing.

In **TheCoachingProgram.com,** one of our clients whom I'll call John said that his wife and brother started playing The Game after they saw positive changes in him. John said that he noticed after a couple weeks into his Game that his wife had completely vacuumed a car that had been sitting in their garage for a long time. He said she had seen him getting things accomplished that he'd never done before and was inspired to take action herself.

All of this communication is good and necessary, but it's not about asking permission from others. You're informing people as graciously as possible that you've made a decision to play The Game and you'd like their support, if they feel they can give it.

R. W. "Butch" Nicholson, the CEO of my company, The Center for Excellence, is a terrific coach and master Game-player. He explains how he prepared his staff prior to playing The Game for the first time.

Butch says:

> *I sat down with people and said, "This is what I'm doing*
> *and what I'm not doing anymore." I figured they'd find ways*
> *to keep up with the velocity while I played The Game. But*
> *I wondered how they'd react to the changes I made at work.*
>
> *It turned out that everybody is happier than they've ever*
> *been. I delegated a lot of tasks to them that I had been doing*
> *so that I could accomplish new things during my Game.*
> *When I come into the office now, they ask me why I'm there.*

Butch may have realized what many others do—people around you have known for a long time that you needed to improve your life. Given the opportunity, most are happy to support your efforts. Life gets better for you *and* for them when you play The Game. Most Game-players have found that if they're in some kind of management position, their staff falls a notch or two below them in applying new behaviors and attitudes. But they *do* follow the leader.

Your Inner Community

As a result of playing The Game, you're in *training* to become a leader. Here's the challenge of The Game's process—the first community you need to lead is the community inside yourself. It's only after getting your inner community in alignment that other people can join and align with you.

The basic elements of structure, affinity, and community apply to your inner, as well as your outer, world. Inside yourself you have a community. There are all sorts of different parts of you that represent your inner community. Some parts of you don't approve of and even criticize other aspects of your personality. What kind of community are you running inside your own internal world? An important factor that will impact your life and performance in The Game is the community of thoughts you live with. There are certain programs you watch on television, or books that you read that are not going to create the fine company you need to produce results. Other images and conversations will inspire you.

You can pull the community of your inner life together by inspiring your mind with a greater good. One of the things I do when I'm feeling a slump and am unmotivated to work out is to watch either the movies *Rocky* or *Chariots of Fire.* I've seen these films a gazillion times, but each viewing shifts the community in my mind, so I regain momentum.

To win at The Game, you'll need to integrate the community inside yourself. Even though you'll never get every part of yourself to agree, you can align behind a higher purpose.

Using Communities for Accountability

Powerfully functional communities hold you accountable for your greatest aspirations. In addition to bringing more resources into your life, community adds accountability. If you're like most of us, it's a challenge to motivate yourself. You're faced with the contradiction that the same self who has been making all the excuses about why you're not accomplishing certain goals in life is now attempting to convince yourself to get moving. It's unlikely that self-motivation is going to work for you. But when you make a commitment to others, you'll become accountable to them and more likely to live up to what you say you want in your life.

Many of you may have played team sports when you were in school. Do you remember the difference in your energy level back then? Wasn't it easier to get yourself to work out, lift weights, and run those miles when you were playing for the *team* and not just for yourself? Teams hold you accountable. Each member has to pull his or her own weight by developing the necessary skills and strength to support a winning team. If you slack off, your team knows about it, and you let people down.

One of the biggest ways in which human beings prevent themselves from producing results is by not making themselves accountable to a team or community. They're secretive about their goals. It's their fail-safe game. They fail because success is an option. They didn't tell their goals to anyone, so nobody can hold them accountable.

One of the basic rules of The Game is:
You only fail by not playing The Game for 90 days.

By enlisting the support of your community, you can deny yourself the option of quitting and not accomplishing what you've always wanted to do.

The People Who See You More Fully

At the end of the evening, I like to read a book to my ten-year-old daughter, Georgia. But sometimes while I'm reading, I'm thinking about my day or all the things I still must do before bedtime. I'm present enough to be able to read the words in the book and say them out loud because it doesn't take a whole lot of my attention to do that much.

One night when I was going through this absentminded routine, Georgia took the book away from me and said, "Make up a story, Daddy."

I found myself stammering, "What do you mean, make up a story? You can't just make up a story."

She said, "Yes, you can. Just make up a story."

I then found myself weaving an incredible tale for my daughter. I became so focused and absorbed in our interaction that, as opposed to my usual read-a-book-for-five-minutes routine,

I stayed with her for about half an hour. By the end of the story, I felt energized, as opposed to how tired I usually was when I distractedly meandered.

Georgia had made me use my full potential as a storyteller *and* as a father. By asking me to make up the story, I had to focus on her. She'd instinctively pushed the book out of my hand and forced me to relate to her. This opened up an opportunity for me to attend to her and to be an excellent parent.

The communities of your children, co-workers, friends, or spouse give you constant opportunities to live up to your full potential. Maybe they're complaining, pulling on your sleeve, or causing disruption. The Game will show you that absolutely every aspect of your life offers a chance to win the life you've always wanted. But if you view the communities that are crying for your attention as distractions, you'll lose the opportunity to manifest your own greatness.

You may have forgotten your potential, but that person making demands is saying, as my daughter did, "I believe you have more to offer than you're giving me." That's not simply an act of defiance. It shows trust and belief in *you*. The person who's persistently tugging on your sleeve is seeing more potential in you than you're seeing in yourself.

Are Communities Your Friends?

When you play The Game, you'll be selecting a partner who will coach you, but as an option, you can also find others who want to form a community of Game-players.

Game-player Orville Lerch told me one of the things he valued most about his community in **TheCoachingProgram.**

He says:

> In a typical community, there's a lot of posturing, but when my coaching class got together with our spouses and

significant others for a vacation weekend, what I noticed at this get-together was that because we'd been so honest with each other during The Game, there was no phoniness. It was different from other communities I'm involved with where everyone seems to play a role and wear a mask, and this is the only way you can be accepted by the group.

When you play The Game with others, if you're all playing it for real, you'll form honest communities. Most people think of community as spending time with like-minded people. In The Game, you'll experience your honest communities as something beyond regular friendship and compatibility.

For example, most people would think that if they've joined a French club, then this gives them a community. This club may offer opportunities for learning and even friendship, but you haven't created a highly functional community until you tell the members of the French club what you're trying to do and ask them to help you and hold you accountable.

Make it clear to your community that their role is not to judge, condemn, or ridicule you if you don't do everything you said you were going to do, or you miss your goal by 10 or 20 percent. Instead, you want them to applaud the 80 percent you *did* accomplish. That's the kind of community you want to form around you. Those are *A Relationships,* and you'll want to have lots of them in your communities.

Our Tendency to Avoid Excellent Communities

The weirdest thing most of do is avoid the very people we need to be around. These are the individuals in your community who will truly hold you accountable. This is why you have to get beyond the concept that communities should be composed of people whom you like and who like you.

I *love* my dad, but as a teenager, there were numerous times when I didn't *like* him, especially if we were discussing an issue and had differing points of view. But I'll tell you something. I've always made it a point to keep the company of my father—not because he always agrees with me, but because he always has my higher purpose in mind. In this way, he's a valuable coach for me.

I can't tell you how many times in our coaching program, a client's spouse is his best coach, but he never listens to her. Then he takes a coaching course from a stranger like me who tells him exactly what his spouse has been saying all along. But me he pays attention to! My theory is that this type of person has been unwilling to accept coaching from his spouse, parents, or loved ones because these are the communities that would hold him most accountable.

What a difference it would make if you selected relationships not only on the basis of compatibility, but because the particular community would earnestly support your higher purpose. This is a factor most people don't even consider when establishing relationships. Yet when people share a higher purpose, they become more compatible.

EXERCISE: LONELY, I'M SO LONELY

List at least three accomplishments in your life. Then list three things you've been trying to do but have never succeeded in achieving. Next to each item, write down whether you've worked on the goal alone or with others. For the things you haven't accomplished, start thinking about what communities you could join or form to support you in achieving these aims.

Exercise: What Are Your Communities Supporting?

List three to five skills, habits, attitudes, or behaviors you want to develop in your life. For example, you may want to get up earlier in the morning, practice martial arts, take up gourmet cooking, learn to speak Spanish, get in the habit of reading faster, take vitamins more regularly, or meditate.

Then write three to five skills, habits, attitudes, or behaviors you *don't* want in your life. Examples might be staying up late and watching TV, criticizing others, interrupting people while they're talking, eating too quickly, or neglecting spiritual/meditative pursuits. Next to each of these items, write down the communities that support these unwanted behaviors.

Exercise: Powerful Communities

Begin to think about areas of your life you want to improve in 90 days, and the goals and skills you'll need to achieve them. After you've read Part II, you're going to return to this exercise to complete it. By then, you will have designed your Game Playing Field, with its major areas of improvement; and you will have identified your goals, along with the behaviors, attitudes, and habits that will help you achieve them.

Then you can decide which communities you could join or form to support you in playing The Game for 90 days. Your next step in this exercise will be, if you haven't already done so, to tell these communities about The Game, your purpose, and your goals, so they can encourage you and help you keep the commitments you're making to yourself. It's a good idea to start thinking about what these communities might be right now, so you can jot down notes in your Game journal as ideas occur to you.

✳ ✳ ✳

The next chapter is going to help you discover how to find and articulate what you were always meant to be and do. What is the heartfelt desire, mission, or calling at the core of your being that will motivate you to win your life in 90 days?

✳ ✳ ✳

CHAPTER 5

Purpose

The Game promises to help you identify and start fulfilling the purpose of your life. It unifies and focuses your time, effort, and energy in support of this purpose.

By "purpose," I mean the heartbeat of your life, what you find most essential and important about your existence. Your purpose is the reason you believe you're here on this earth. Your purpose doesn't only occur in the afterlife. It exists *now*, in the midst of chaotic, challenging, mundane daily living.

As you get clearer about your purpose and the meaning life has for you, it's easier to take committed, powerful, immediate action. One of the reasons you hesitate at the threshold of your life is that you're not clear about *why* you're doing something. When you understand the reason for achieving a goal and it's in line with your purpose, you're willing to suffer through almost anything.

One of the very best books on the subject of "purpose" is Viktor Frankl's *Man's Search for Meaning*. The author writes about people in concentration camps whose lack of purpose made them most likely to succumb to death through hardship. A purpose is essential for human beings; it can literally keep them alive.

After you clarify your purpose, you'll have little to no trouble making decisions. You'll always be able to take a look at any set of options and ask: Which one of these choices furthers my purpose to the greatest extent? Without a purpose, you make little, reactionary, noncohesive decisions in the moment, and this leads to a life of compromise rather than decisiveness. Your entire existence ends up being mediocre, because you weren't able to pull yourself together behind a greater good. Knowing your purpose keeps you from contradicting yourself. Without a purpose, you want one thing, then moments later, you want something else. This makes it impossible for you to marshal your forces and produce anything meaningful.

Perhaps Game-player Dean Lampe explained it best. He says, "You're here for a reason. The Game takes a lot of the crap out of your daily life and lets you define and focus all your energies toward that reason."

After you've identified your purpose, there's a whole range of options that opens up to you with respect to how you run your life.

Discovering Your Purpose

Purpose is already in your life as a flicker, if not a roaring flame. You'll be *uncovering* rather than *discovering* it. Purpose lingers like the scent of roses or fine perfume. As you focus your quiet attention on life's heartfelt and reverent moments, your purpose will reveal itself.

Now, see if you can remember some of the most moving times of your life. These are the moments that really spoke to you.

Examples of such instances might be the following:

- The birth of your child
- The first time you entered a classroom to teach or to learn

- The speech you delivered, which got a standing ovation
- The story, song, or poem you wrote that made others laugh or cry
- The joy on the faces of your friends when you cooked a gourmet meal for them
- The time your pet wouldn't leave your side when you were sick or scared
- The day you thought life couldn't get any worse, but a rainbow splashed across the sky and filled you with hope and wonder

Look for moments that moved you so deeply that they've helped to define you. Why did these experiences inspire you so? Others have seen rainbows, written poetry, and cooked meals, yet your reactions to whatever experiences have popped into your mind were profound. Let these moments speak to you now. Moving, poignant, memorable experiences point you in the direction of your purpose.

What Do You Love?

Next, consider what you love. When you think about your daily life, what acts do you find yourself looking forward to? What do you love to see, feel, touch, taste, or smell? The things in life that naturally cause you to feel love unlock the mystery of your purpose, because purpose arises from a loving heart.

Game-player Jeanne Stilwell found that playing The Game helped her get into closer alignment with her purpose by allowing her to excel at what she loves to do. Jeanne says, "Of all the life changes that occurred in 90 days, the most notable was how I did public speaking. When presenting, I began looking into the

eyes of a participant for a thought and making an unbeliev-
ably enriched connection with the audience." Jeanne was tap-
ping into the full potential of one who fulfills her dreams by creating rapport and communicating ideas.

Paying close attention to what may seem like the mundane or inconsequential things you love—listening to great
music, working in your garden, playing with the dog—can give
you more clarity about what your purpose might be. Observing
what you love can even lead you into a line of work or career
path that is more aligned with your purpose.

A woman I know believes that her purpose is to bring beauty
into the lives of everyone she meets. One thing she noticed
about herself is that she loves to shop. Her affinity for shopping
led her to become a personal shopper. She genuinely enjoys
helping her clients look and feel beautiful in the clothes she
advises them to select.

Purpose doesn't exist in the abstract. It gives real definition
to your daily life by prompting you to fulfill its promise. If you
tell me that your purpose is to serve children, but you never
spend time with any kids, then this must not be your true purpose. If it was, your love for children would be consistently
drawing them naturally into your life.

Another way to reveal your purpose, related to what you
love, is to look at your life's accomplishments. What do you
do well without giving much thought to it? You probably consider these skills to be inclinations or proclivities. You think
they're genetic, innate, or natural talents. Yet, these gifts are
strongly related to the reason why you're here. These natural
abilities help you manifest your purpose.

Learn from the Purpose of Others

Here's another way to discover your purpose. Ask people
you meet—even strangers—what they think their purpose is.

Their responses may contain seeds that will trigger thoughts and ideas about your own purpose.

Here's the simple question I've asked: *What is your purpose?* I've posed it to cab drivers, bellhops, and high-powered business executives. I've been amazed to watch people's faces brighten as they've answered this question. Many can't quite articulate their purpose. As I've mentioned, this is something you tend to formulate and deepen over time. But many of the strangers I've casually asked about their purpose talk about their children, and although many of them can't distill the principle behind the examples they give, I can read between the lines and see that they do have a purpose.

By asking this question of others, you'll also raise the level of dialogue in the world as you remind people that there is a purpose to their lives.

Writing Your Statement of Purpose

Don't rush the process of defining and expressing your purpose. Developing a statement about your purpose takes thought and attention. As you continue to read this book, work through the exercises, and most important, play The Game, you can refine your statement of purpose. When you graduate from having a vague notion to a very clearly articulated statement of purpose, this produces clarity in your life.

After you've written the first draft of your purpose statement, post it everywhere to remind you and others what it is. Share your statement of purpose with your communities. I've even see people put their purpose statements after their names on e-mails. Embrace your purpose. It will inform and enrich all you do, say, feel, believe, and think.

Here is my own statement of purpose, which shapes and is an expression of this book:

> *Everywhere I go, I will engage people in a level of dialogue that makes them present to their own greatness, and thereby facilitates peace and deepens love for all humans for all time.*

The Difference Between Aligning and Agreeing

One of the challenges in The Game (and in life) is to get the different parts of yourself to align, as opposed to forcing every aspect of yourself to agree. A friend of mine who was considering starting a diet program for her Game tells how she used the principle of alignment versus agreement to make a decision. She says:

> *I wanted to lose weight during my 90-day Game. This served my purpose well because I need to be healthier to fulfill it. I was considering which diet program to use since I've tried almost anything you could mention at one time or another. Then I remembered that two friends told me they'd lost 20 or more pounds on a program that has prepackaged foods, a once-a-week weigh-in, and is very simple for a busy person like me to use.*
>
> *My next thought was that using prepackaged foods would go against my current standard of eating mostly organic and unprocessed foods. I was about to give up on the idea of this weight-loss program, when I remembered what Sarano always says about getting alignment rather than pushing for agreement. One part of me wanted the convenience of the packaged foods and weekly weigh-in. Another part was a purist about organics.*
>
> *Then I thought, What would best serve my purpose?*

Immediately, the solution came to mind. Of course I'm not going to die if I eat processed food for 90 days. This program also includes salads, fruits, and vegetables, which I can buy organic. Losing weight and gaining the momentum of having my health back in 90 days definitely serves my purpose. After the 90 days, I'll eat organically as exclusively as possible—only I'll be eating less of these foods.

The beauty of knowing your purpose is that all of you, even the disagreeable parts, will align behind it. This enables you to gather tremendous velocity in The Game, because you'll spend less time arguing and fighting against yourself and be more able to take action.

Higher Purpose

You'll notice that the purpose statements I've chosen to share with you in this book are far beyond personal fulfillment and individual concerns. These are examples of what I call a *higher* purpose. The more expansive your purpose is, the more effective it tends to be. When you have a higher purpose, it inspires others to help you fulfill it.

A higher purpose usually causes you to stretch further than you could have imagined yourself going. There's an adage that says: *Get a big problem, and you'll get a big life.* When a higher purpose leads, you create miracles in your own life and the lives of others. When you play The Game and connect all the dots of your life with your higher purpose, that's a game worth playing.

One of the questions I pose in **TheCoachingProgram.com** classes relates to how much time our clients are taking to work for their higher purpose. At first, their answer is: "Very little time at all." Those people realize that they're dragging along from day to day, earning a living and hoping to survive. That process of not working for your higher purpose and merely getting through life is what I call *Working for The Man.*

Then there are the people who work in service all of their lives. Their presence on this planet is a blessing to others. Many individuals who give such service do so without recognition and often aren't appreciated until after they die. They may be occupying the same jobs as those who work for The Man, but they keep their higher purpose in mind and fulfill their responsibilities differently.

I remember listening to one of my coaching clients who's in the financial services industry talking about his higher purpose. He said that living in alignment with the meaning of his life and focusing on service had caused him to begin handling his own clients in a new and even more compassionate way. He'd started asking them what kind of service they want to provide for humanity with their wealth, even after their death. He asked them to consider what their legacy would be—not exactly the standard fare of portfolio analysis.

But most of us aren't like my coaching client. We spend our lives simply slaving for The Man. There's nothing wrong with bondage; it's a choice like any other. I'd just prefer not to be a slave, thank you.

I usually end my conversation about The Man with a slogan that helps my clients remember why they hit levels of resistance when they play The Game. I explain that when you're free of bondage and start aligning with your higher purpose, the people and things to which you've always given over your power are likely to protest. As my coaching clients start to have breakthroughs in this regard, I often tease them by saying, "The Man isn't going to like that."

I suspect that The Man isn't going to like this book at all!

✶ ✶ ✶

The Difference Between a Purpose and an Issue

After you write your initial statement of purpose, see if it is in any way divisive, uncompromising, rigid, exclusive, unloving, or setting you up *against* instead of *for* humanity. If so, it's probably an issue, not a purpose. Issues tend to create dividing lines between people.

I have a friend I love dearly. He's very committed to Jesus Christ, yet he pushes his beliefs onto people and drives them away. This is his *issue*, not his *purpose*. It's like the person who stops smoking and becomes a cigarette cop. He's making his issue with smoking take on a life beyond what it needs to be.

A purpose unites people, while causes have a tendency to divide us. Causes have sides that people are for or against. Purposes aren't necessarily *against* anything but are *for* the well-being of a larger community.

I didn't write this book for a cause. It serves a higher purpose. My writing of this book, your reading of it, and the playing of The Game are honorable things to do.

Honor

Honor very simply means operating in accord with your purpose. One of the most important things you'll learn in The Game is that to honor your word means to honor yourself. If you keep your commitments, your word becomes law in your own universe and has power. In an interview for this book, Game-player Mary Wichmann made a simple but profound statement that sums up what honor can do in your life. She said, "The Game restored the power of my word. Everyone, including me, now knows that I do what I say I'm going to do."

There's a reverence and sacredness in honor. It's so much more than duty and responsibility. Honor is about making powerful, though difficult, choices. This is also the nature of The

Game. As you consistently honor your purpose, it begins to take on a life of its own. Even when you don't think you're doing anything, you'll continue to manifest what you want to accomplish.

The End of Regret

Living an honorable life leads to dying with honor. It's not enough at the final moment to reconcile yourself to your higher purpose. When you're lying on your deathbed, it's much too late for regret, yet look how many people live their entire lives filled with disappointment or guilt.

See if you can answer this powerful question: *What do I need to do so that I can die without regret?* You'll find that regrets spring directly from not fulfilling your purpose. When the people I've taught and coached have answered this question, it has created profound changes in their lives.

You regret the times when you did things halfheartedly. Rarely have I seen a person give something their all and have regrets. You regret not powerfully committing to your last relationship. You regret not performing at a high level on your last job. You regret not fully expressing love for your parents before they died.

By getting clear about what you would need to do to die without regret, you have the opportunity to die with honor, to exit your life gratefully, and view eternity as a well-deserved rest from life's long labors. The combination of purpose, honor, and living without regret produces an incredible sense of inner power.

Your Eulogy

What if you were to write your own eulogy right now while you're still alive? Do you know what you'd want to say about yourself? At first, it may seem morbid to write about your life as if it has already passed. But in a sense, it *has*. What you'd bury by writing your eulogy now is the life you've lived so far, that one that's probably filled with regrets.

It was a good life in many ways. You touched many people. This eulogy will likely contain the kindest words you've ever said about and to yourself.

To manifest your purpose, you have to stop criticizing yourself. Writing your eulogy gives you the opportunity to start a new conversation. You're burying your sense of immortality. You're accepting the fact that "later" and "someday" are *now*. By formally acknowledging the life you've lived so far, you become present to how important it is to use your gifts and resources to create—with the help of the 90-day Game—the life you've always wanted.

Leslie Hidaka delivered his eulogy in one of our coaching program classes. He says this exercise had a profound influence on him and helped him to understand The Game and his life more deeply.

He writes:

I understood the following concepts IN MY BONES:

- *It's my life, and it's ALL up to me.*
- *There's a bigger picture, the universe, something else at work that I'd forgotten during my little dilemmas.*
- *In the scope of things, the conversation I was having with myself was petty and irrelevant. I was wasting my time and energy thinking about it.*
- *I can choose freely how I want to live my life.*

What was available for me [by writing my eulogy] was freedom, presence, and love. I had compassion for myself and got very clear on the insignificance of me, my mind, my feelings, and my little world. What I have now is complete and total freedom to live my life, moment by moment, making choices every day without reasons or justifications. I don't think about, analyze, regret, change, worry, or obsess about my choices. They are just choices. I get to live EXACTLY how I choose. WOW!

PURPOSEFUL EXERCISES

Review what we've discussed in Part I, and do the activities I've described to help you discover and fulfill your purpose:

- Identify your most memorable moments.

- Ask others, "What is your purpose?" Listen to their answers for clues to your own purpose.

- Identify what you love to do.

- Write a first draft of your statement of purpose.

- Expand your purpose to a higher level that serves all life.

- Analyze your goals to see where you could get internal alignment behind your purpose, even if you can't get all the parts of yourself to agree.

- Write in your Game journal what you think you need to do to die with honor and without regret.

- Write your eulogy in your Game journal. Read it to others to make it an even more powerful experience.

✳ ✳ ✳

Congratulations! You've finished reading Part I of this book. You're on your way to winning your life!

If I were to predict whether this book and The Game would make a dent in your life and in the world, even with its substantial prizes, I might set some rather low (others would call "realistic") expectations. It's a fact that most people don't take powerful action. My expectations might be that you'll read this book and say, "Oh, yeah, right," and go on with life as it is. Or, you'll think you already know all the information in the book and don't need to play The Game.

But The Game and this book are designed to go beyond *your, my,* and *our* collective expectations. So now I'll tell you what I really think will happen.

I believe that you're going to read this book, do the exercises, register to play The Game, and have 90 of the most remarkable days of your life.

Now I'll tell you what I really, really expect to happen— *far* beyond the usual expectations that an author can hope for when writing a book.

I sincerely believe that playing The Game will become a national and then an international phenomenon. You'll be sitting in restaurants and coffee shops or standing in movie and grocery store lines overhearing people ask each other: *Are you playing The Game? How many points do you have? What's your higher purpose? How can I help you fulfill it?*

People everywhere will play The Game and support each other openly and willingly. Companies and individuals will offer products, services, and prizes to inspire people to play The Game in the aspects of life they've chosen to focus on for 90 days. This book's readers will meet each other through **TheGameInteractive.com** Website, and some will form local Game-playing groups. Entire corporations and cities will play The Game to win the life of their organizations and communities. They'll align behind a higher purpose that encompasses their individual purpose, and find new and creative ways to offer service to all life. When people worldwide are playing The Game to win their lives, this will bring about a renaissance in consciousness.

So, right now, I'm urging you to be THE ONE who goes beyond all my expectations.

I challenge you to win your life.

I challenge you to take back your life from your own critical, negative thoughts.

I challenge you to take back your life from the people who don't believe you can do it.

I challenge you to find joy in the unexpected pleasure of exceeding all your expectations as you learn in Part II about the life it's possible to win while you're playing The Game!

✷ ✷ ✷

★ PART II ★

What Aspects of Your Life Do You Want to Improve?

"After I played The Game for a while, it didn't take me long to realize that all the old struggles and issues were still around, but the way I was viewing and responding to each challenge had changed. Nothing seemed to be as big a deal as it had been in the past. I wasn't as anxious and uptight. I started taking time to meditate and pray, and I felt more relaxed. One evening after I was almost finished with my 90 days, I took my children out to dinner. I mentioned to them that I was coming to the end of playing The Game. My son looked at me and said, 'Dad, you're more understanding now.' My daughter said, 'Dad, you're more gentle.'"

— **Gary Schell, Player of The Game**

★ CHAPTER 6 ★

Balance

I f you're like most of us, you're playing many roles and have a multitude of aspects to your life. In addition, there are many areas of human endeavor you've seen others engaging in, know are possible, or sound intriguing, but haven't begun to explore. Playing The Game is going to help you find the delicate balance required for discovering new territory, while maintaining a truly satisfying life.

It's easy to lose balance in your day and in your life. Competing demands—whatever is making the most noise, falling apart fastest, or fulfilling your immediate needs—scramble for your attention. Before you realize it, your life is crowded into only a few rooms where the greatest crises are occurring, instead of allowing you to explore and develop the many facets of human existence.

Before you play The Game, you're going to rate your effectiveness at the many roles you're currently playing. You'll discover where you're playing only one or two notes, when you could be performing a symphony. As you design and play your Game, you'll figure out how to balance your time and other resources while fulfilling your purpose.

Your Many Roles

First, let's take a look at the ways in which you're like some frantic actor playing on other people's stages as well as your own. You may simultaneously be a parent, spouse, significant other, sibling, advisor, co-worker, manager (even if only of yourself), sports team coach, scout leader, deacon in your church—the list goes on endlessly.

Look at any one of these roles, and break it down into components. As part of just one job, you might fill the role of friend, counselor, clerk, analyst, supervisor, trainer, coffee-maker, fashion trendsetter, and meeting planner. At home, you could be a wife, mother, housemaid, repair person, cook, laundress, household organizer, manager, and chauffeur. Whew!

How well are you performing these roles? Do you have more affinity for some than others? As you think about yourself in each role, where do you notice a dip in your effectiveness?

Balance in all of life is an essential ingredient for health and success. Game-player Greg Kadet explains that balance is a skill he wanted to acquire while playing The Game, but it also became part of his higher purpose.

He writes:

> I identified the areas that I wanted to improve during The Game. I was going to be married in seven days, so I put my fiancée and our relationship at the top of my list. Then I decided on the other areas that were most important to me. After about 60 days into The Game, I started to get an idea of what my higher purpose was. I realized that I'm here to become a balanced man. My life isn't about being proficient in one thing or another. I don't want to be like a lot of people who only do a couple things very well, and everything else in their lives is in shambles. I want to be totally balanced in all things.

The Major Areas of Life

Here in Part II, we'll focus on the major areas of your life. In Part III, after you've analyzed the possible areas of life to target for improvement, you'll design your Game's Playing Field. Each chapter in Part II will go into more detail about major areas of life and prepare you with special Game rules and exercises for accomplishing your goals.

In The Game, you'll be taking on the challenge of multi-dimensional living. You'll measure your accomplishments before and after playing The Game. In the essays you and your partner send to me, you'll write down how you've achieved stunning and dramatic results. I'll be looking for ways in which you were able to achieve balance while playing a variety of roles. Improving three to five areas of life at once in only 90 days creates an extraordinary level of focus, discipline, and clarity. Focusing on multiple areas simultaneously is designed to help you get out of control. That probably sounds contradictory, because I've said that The Game helps you manage your life better.

Ultimately, it does, but as you begin the process of playing, you'll probably feel your life spinning at a whole new level of velocity. Game-player Mary Wichmann explains how The Game provided her with a new perspective on her need for control.

She writes:

> *I learned by playing The Game that I can't control time. I can't always control what happens. I can't control everything. I have learned to deal with life as it comes, to "go with the flow," to be present to life as it occurs, instead of trying to have everything under my perfect management. This is what The Game ultimately came to be about for me.*
>
> *The velocity I picked up while playing made me get out of my normal routines, and I noticed that I was beginning to trust myself and life more.*

One day I was rushing home. As I zipped out of town, I saw the last gas station I'd be coming to for another ten miles. I don't know why, but I just thought to look at my fuel tank, and that's when I noticed that the gas gauge was on empty. This isn't something that ever happens to me. I'm not the type of person who runs out of gas. I'd been so busy getting everything accomplished for The Game that I hadn't even checked the fuel level in my car.

What occurred to me, though, is that I DID get a reminder inside of myself to look at the gauge at exactly the time when I really needed to think about it. This incident gave me a level of trust I'd never had. I realized I could ride within the flow of life without having to consciously be in control of everything.

We live in times when we're encouraged to be idiot savants. It's as if we're taught to only sing one song that we repeat often enough to convince ourselves that this is the only music worth hearing. Our modern-day behavior is very different from the Renaissance era, where people were encouraged to become proficient and interested in a multitude of interests. The nature of a Renaissance is having people exhibit a high degree of excellence in many fields of human endeavor. We're going for a Renaissance by introducing The Game throughout the world. We're going for excellence by promoting the sorely neglected skill of leading a balanced life.

EXERCISE: WHAT ARE YOU *REALLY* UP TO?

First, think about the roles you play in your family, business, community, country, and the world. (For example, you may simultaneously be a parent, spouse, child, sibling, advisor, youth sports team coach, deacon in your church, etc.). On separate lines of your Game journal, list the top ten roles you play in your life currently. Leave a blank space after each role.

Next, rank your current effectiveness in each of these roles using a percentage scale from 0 percent to 100 percent.

Now, answer the following questions in your Game journal:

- In which roles are you least effective?

- Would you like to improve your skills, efficiency, and satisfaction with the lowest ranking roles? Why or why not?

- Are there ways you could combine some of these roles?

- When you start playing The Game, could you delegate, reassign, or share with others certain duties within these roles?

- Are there roles you don't need to improve but could entirely eliminate from your responsibilities?

Later, you'll be able to design your Game Playing Field so that you can learn to excel at these roles in the next 90 days.

✶ ✶ ✶

If you're like many people, one of the top priorities for your Game will be in the area of physical fitness and health. In the next chapter, you'll read inspirational stories and get great tips for handling this aspect of life. You'll discover ways to develop the habits, skills, and attitudes you've always wanted so you can live with as much vitality and energy as possible.

✶ ✶ ✶

★ CHAPTER 7 ★

Your Body and Health

Playing The Body and Health Game is an Olympic event, and its gold-medal prize is winning a healthy body and lifestyle. We probably "should" ourselves more when it comes to physical fitness than in any other aspect of life. We *should* lose weight. We *should* get buffed. We *should* take better care of our bodies. We *should* go for therapy. We *should* join a health club. This seemingly endless list tends to keep us frozen in a state of inaction—until something goes drastically wrong with our health.

Playing The Body and Health Game is going to end all your waiting, procrastinating, and indecision. You'll find that having a healthy and energetic body allows you to place a greater emphasis on everything else that you want to accomplish in life.

Preparing for The Body and Health Game

The Body and Health Game is designed to help you focus your time and attention on physical and mental fitness. To begin, you'll need to assess how physically fit you are so that you can deal with your health issues in 90 days.

The first thing to do is to gather data using as many of the following methods as you can, and post the results on your Before-and-After Displays.

Consider getting a checkup that includes the following:

- A complete physical by a doctor
- Mammogram, cholesterol level, colon, and/or bone density tests
- Nutrition and diet analysis
- Body fat percentage analysis
- A dental exam
- A mental-health evaluation (if you want to make mental health part of your Game).

If you're not able at this time to get a complete physical due to lack of insurance or other financial issues, seek out as much information about your body as you possibly can. Most major cities have organizations that sponsor free or inexpensive mammogram tests. For example, look in the Yellow Pages under the heading "Mammography." Call organizations and ask for information on where screenings for uninsured people are conducted in your area. You can also call the American Cancer Society at 1-800-237-2345 to get help.

Having your blood pressure checked is as easy as testing yourself at machines installed in many pharmacies, grocery stores, and discount department stores. You can buy a scale at a bathroom-fixture store that calculates both your weight and percentage of body fat. Be creative, and you'll find ways to get the baseline data you need to measure your progress in The Body and Health Game.

The fundamental problem with not having regular physical exams is that health issues that could have been detected earlier later show up as emergencies, robbing you of time and energy. Health problems often recur because you haven't dealt with them at their source. Maybe you haven't taken the time to find out why you lack energy, gain weight easily, or frequently get colds. Before you're in crisis is the best time to make your health a top priority.

Game-player Bess Turner had an astounding journey that resulted just from getting a physical checkup before playing The Body and Health Game.

She writes:

> *I have a family history of colon cancer and was supposed to be screened ten years ago. I chickened out twice, once the night before the procedure. This time, before playing The Game, I went for the test and found out that I was okay.*
>
> *I knew I needed surgery for fibroid tumors. A week after I started playing The Game, a physical exam revealed that I had to have a potentially dangerous, tennis-ball size cyst removed. Five weeks before the surgery was scheduled, during my pre-op exam, my doctor did another sonogram but couldn't find the cyst. She looked at me incredulously and said, "You healed yourself."*
>
> *I'm not sure if this miracle was the result of my Game partner Al Dogger's relentless prayers on my behalf, but I certainly think it contributed, and I appreciated his concern for my health. In any event, it wasn't "medically possible" for the cyst to disappear, but it happened during the 90 days that I was playing The Game.*

A special rule for The Body and Health Game is:
Get as complete a physical checkup as possible before
and after playing for 90 days.

✳ ✳ ✳

What to Expect

People from my coaching classes who have played The Body and Health Game have lost as much as 30 pounds in 90 days. I've found it amazing to see the transformations that are possible when people consistently and wholeheartedly develop healthy practices and habits. But things don't always happen exactly as we think they should.

Game-player Loy Gotham writes:

> I was diligently working at my health program and eating carefully. To my surprise, I gained two pounds after starting to exercise! I didn't know what to do, so I kept plugging along. About ten days later, after I'd weighed in two pounds heavier, I was getting undressed and noticed that I was buckling my belt two notches smaller than usual. I ran to the scale to see if I'd lost anything, but I weighed the same as the previous week.
>
> A month later, after continuing with my new health regimen, I had my percentage of body fat rechecked. I was very surprised to discover that of the weight I'd lost, 40 percent of it was body fat.
>
> After 90 days, my body felt much more toned. I was stronger and could lift heavier weights. My clothes were fitting looser, so I knew I had made progress, but the needle on my scale didn't seem to want to budge.

I like this story because it shows how persistence pays off in unexpected ways. Loy applied the basic Game rule that you can only lose The Game by *not* playing for 90 days.

Dean Lampe says:

> I'm 6'3", and I weighed 203 pounds when I started playing The Game. For 90 days, I carefully watched what I ate, worked out five days a week, did push-ups and sit-ups, lifted

my luggage when I traveled, and ran up and down steps in hotels. I never went to a gym. I just worked out with whatever was available in my immediate surroundings and substantially increased my daily activity. At the end of The Game, I'd brought my body fat down to 11 percent, and I weighed 179 pounds. This is the best shape I've been in since college.

By the way, don't procrastinate about playing The Body and Health Game while you search for the "right" diet. The Game offers you the opportunity to experiment intelligently and discover what produces results for you.

Balance and Multitasking

Here are some practical multitasking suggestions for playing The Body and Health Game and increasing your level of activity and metabolism while improving or not neglecting other areas of your life:

- When someone wants to meet with you, ask if the two of you can walk while you talk.
- Have meetings with colleagues at the gym while you're walking side-by-side on the treadmills.
- Lift hand weights while you're waiting for *anything*, such as when your computer is booting up or while your morning coffee is percolating.
- Do stretches at your desk; hold in your abdominal muscles while driving or sitting.

A special rule for The Body and Health Game is:
Multitask in order to make improvements in your health blend in with the other things you're doing in The Game.

Scoring Your Body and Health Game Points

Refer to Part III for explanations of each of The Game's basic elements. You'll use the special rules and goals you've set for The Body and Health Game, and give yourself points for doing what you've committed to, or take away points for not doing what you said you would.

Game-Player Stephen Masri says:

> *The idea of starting an exercise program was sort of daunting. But I broke it down into its achievable components. I knew that I could do things like taking a half-hour vigorous walk or doing a set number of push-ups and sit-ups. So I scheduled certain times every day when I did those small amounts of exercise and gave myself points each time I kept appointments with myself.*

During her 90-day Body and Health Game, Mary Wichmann lost 25 pounds, including 10 pounds of body fat. She mentions some of the items for which she gave herself points.

Mary says:

> *I acquired a real appreciation for exercise while playing The Game. This is no longer something I have to do. I actually look forward to it. I gave myself points for walking the steps instead of taking the elevator, biking instead of driving my car; and balancing proteins, carbohydrates, and fats at each meal. I've resumed the practice of T'ai Chi, and scored a point each time I met with my instructor.*
>
> *For the first time in my life, my driver's license overstates my weight by ten pounds.*

Be sure to include as part of your points and goals whatever principles are part of the diet, exercise, or health system you've chosen to use for 90 days.

A special rule for The Body and Health Game is:
Break larger goals into small tasks and behaviors
that you can give yourself points for, and reward
yourself for achieving.

Structure, Affinity, and Community for Body-Health Games

There are many structures you can design to win The Body and Health Game. Something that has worked well for me is Bill Phillips's 90-day program for increasing physical fitness. You can read about it in his book *Body for Life* (HarperCollins, 1999), or visit his Website at: **www.eas.com.**

I've also enjoyed the structure of taking hatha yoga classes. I find that this 5,000-year-old practice of yoga, with its emphasis on breathing deeply, stretching, twisting, and moving slowly is great for reducing stress and increasing energy. In 1990, after Dr. Dean Ornish wrote about the benefits of yoga in the respected medical journal *Lancet,* the medical community began to take notice of yoga's effectiveness in reversing heart disease, lowering high blood pressure, stimulating digestion, and managing stress.

Other types of structures can include the following:

- Joining a health and fitness club (or a YMCA or YWCA)
- Hiring a personal trainer
- Getting books, videos, or magazines explaining how to use the diet or exercise program or system you've chosen
- Taking exercise or nutrition classes
- Enrolling in an exercise and diet program or club

To acquire an affinity for The Body and Health Game, you'd want to find a partner, coach, friend, or acquaintance who loves to do whatever *you* find difficult to do. Affinity partners or coaches can include those who:

- work out regularly with vigor and enthusiasm,
- have lost weight, body fat, and strengthened their muscles through diet and exercise,
- incorporate relaxation and stress-relieving methods into their daily lives, and
- have had health issues similar to yours but have found ways to overcome them.

To form and find communities that will assist you in The Body and Health Game, you might join classes, support groups, and organizations devoted to health and fitness.

Game-player Greg Kadet combined all three basic elements of the Game—structure, affinity, and community—when he played to win his health.

Greg says:

> *My greatest accomplishment while playing The Game was that I ran a ten-mile race, and I've never been a jogger in my entire life. In fact, I despise running. But now I'm training with a partner* [structure and affinity] *to run a charity marathon* [structure, affinity, and community]. *This means that I'm jogging 30 to 40 miles a week. I've even become passionate about jogging* [affinity].

Rewards, Consequences, and Deadlines

How often have you been the taskmaster without ever being the party-giver for yourself? How many of your goals have you discarded and failed to achieve because you didn't give yourself the kind of caring and self-acknowledgment we all need?

How flimsy and noncommittal have you been because you haven't given yourself any deadlines or consequences for not achieving your goals?

When playing The Body and Health Game, you need to reward yourself regularly for accomplishing goals and for scoring high numbers of points. Just remember not to select rewards that move you in the opposite direction of achieving your goals. If you were trying to lose inches and you did, don't reward yourself with a milkshake. Instead, give yourself the treat of having a massage or buying yourself a present of some sort.

To play The Game most effectively, you can administer funny but humiliating consequences for not keeping commitments to yourself. For example, you could set a goal that on day 45 you'll be walking or running three miles each day. If you haven't reached that goal, you'll carry a watermelon everywhere you go for three days in a row, including work, movies, church, and restaurants. When people ask you why you're walking around with a watermelon, you have to answer, "Because this is how much extra weight I'm carrying on my body, and I'm not walking/running three miles a day yet even though I said I would." This should open up many "fruitful" conversations and increase your motivation to achieve this goal right away.

Special Tips, Skills, and Rules

I'm offering ideas to stimulate your thinking and inspire you to acquire healthy habits and behaviors. My suggestions come from my own personal experiences and those of others who have played The Game. It takes commitment to play The Body and Health Game, but 70-year-old Game-player George Page holds up the standard for all of us.

George says:

I used to be a runner, but I gave it up because I was too old, and my feet couldn't handle running. To play The Game, I hired a personal trainer, and this guy made me stretch my boundaries. He had me doing things I've never done before. It got me into better physical shape than I've been in, in 20 years.

To make running more fun and challenging for myself, I started to run around my neighborhood every which way. I ran forward, backwards, sideways, and zigzag. My trainer said I'd be safer doing this crazy running style in a gym, but I told him I'm the kind of person who needs to be outdoors.

It helped that I ran at five or six in the morning, while it was still dark and my neighbors couldn't see me. They think I'm an odd guy anyway. But one day, some kids were waiting for their school bus and were watching me. They all turned around and didn't take their eyes off me while I ran down the street. I waved at them, and they waved back. To play The Game, it helps if you're willing to be a little different.

A special rule for The Body and Health Game is:
Increase the amount of physical exercise you do every day.

Your Body Knows and Tells

By playing The Body and Health Game, you'll have the chance to really focus on what your body is trying to tell you. Is your body letting you know that you require more rest? Need more physical activity? Require certain foods to be in or out of your diet? Does your body give certain signals for when it's full, hungry, or thirsty? Listening to your body will help you detect all the subtle clues you've been ignoring while your attention has been on anything and everything else but your health.

A special rule for The Body and Health Game is:
Listen to your body.

Taste Bud Alert

Remember the principle of alignment versus agreement. Your sense of taste may never agree with what's best for the rest of your body. Just remind yourself that *tasting* good doesn't always translate into *being* good for you.

One of the habits I use to keep my taste buds in alignment with my health goals is to decide what I want to eat, based on the diet or nutrition plan I'm using, *before* I ever look at the menu in a restaurant. Then I check to see if the restaurant serves what I want. If it doesn't, I'm one of those people who politely but firmly requests a special order. In most cases, I get what I want merely by asking for it. I'm also careful to order my vegetables steamed instead of fried, and to ask that sauces, gravies, and other delicious "gooeys" not even be put on my plate.

A special rule for The Body and Health Game is:
Don't let your taste buds rule.

Keeping a Food Diary

I also listen to my body by periodically keeping a food diary for a period of time. I compare my energy level with the foods I'm eating. Then I can make connections between foods that decrease my vitality and those that help me stay energetic.

A special rule for The Body and Health Game is:
Periodically keep a food diary.

I also engage in the practice of *grazing* by eating small meals or snacks up to six or ten times a day at regular intervals. By doing so, my body never feels full or hungry. I reduce my calorie intake by evening when I'm less active.

I once heard that those 400-pound Sumo wrestlers only eat once a day, late in the day. Then they go to sleep immediately after eating. This is not too different from the kind of diet many of us follow. We're Sumo wrestlers-in-the-making. According to some experts, when your body learns that it can't depend on regular intervals of food, it slows the metabolic process and stores fat to make sure you don't starve. If you diet and then starve yourself, you trigger your body's starvation mechanisms, deplete your energy, and potentially damage your health. The only way you'll be able to accurately understand your body's rhythms and needs is to observe yourself in relation to food.

To keep my body fine-tuned, as often as possible I drink a gallon of water each day. Water washes out toxins, aids digestion, and keeps the stomach feeling full.

Another special rule for The Body and Health Game is: *Drink at least eight 8-ounce glasses of water each day.*

How Much Sleep Do You Need?

My fellow Game-players and I have had some interesting revelations about how much sleep we really need while playing The Game. Some of us have decreased the number of hours we sleep by nearly 50 percent. Others have discovered that they need even *more* sleep and started taking short naps during the day to give themselves mid-morning or mid-afternoon respites. I'm not advocating sleep deprivation; I'm just raising the possibility that you may be getting more sleep than you need, and during The Game, you can experiment with these options.

Have you noticed yourself sleeping through the night and

then, early in the morning, beginning to wake up? For me, this happens quite frequently at about 4:00 A.M.

Try getting out of bed when your body delivers a natural wake-up call instead of waiting for the alarm to ring. Many Game-players find that the excitement and fun of this remarkable 90-day adventure causes them to spring out of bed and look forward to embracing the challenges they've set for themselves.

If you resist life, your tendency will be to go back to sleep and tell yourself that you'll be tired if you get up early. In contrast, if you embrace life and let yourself awaken naturally to it, your mind will be fully rested and imbued with energy and power. If you roll over and go back to sleep, you may find that this is when you have your most energy-draining dreams. Every single time you hit the snooze button on your alarm clock, you'll feel more and more tired. By the time you do get up, you'll be thrown off balance by too much sleep and won't be able to regain momentum.

Of course, the additional benefit of having extra early morning hours is that they're treasures of quiet, personal time for physical exercise, meditation, prayer, journal writing, and any activities that are best done without interruption and distraction. Early rising helps you do those valuable *A Activities* with an *A Relationship*—you.

You may also find that by playing The Game and staying focused on your higher purpose and goals that you reduce your amount of daydreaming. I've noticed that the less people daydream, the less sleep they need at night. The more that the mind is kept busy with purposeful thoughts and activities during the day, the deeper and more restful sleep is at night.

Often people sleep a lot because they're depressed. The nature of The Game is to relieve depression with meaningful and powerful action. Again, this can result in the need for less sleep.

A special rule for The Body and Health Game is:
Get up when you wake up.

THE BODY AND HEALTH GAME EXERCISE

Use the activities that go with the special rules and Game elements described above if you decide to make the Body and Health Game one of the three to five aspects of life you want to improve in 90 days. Design The Body and Health Game by using The Game's basic elements described in Part III of this book: goals, To-Be and Not-To-Be lists, points, prizes, rules, Before-and-After Displays, essays, skills, rewards, consequences, deadlines, partners, and coaches. Refer to **TheGameInteractive.com** Website for more ideas and coaching specifically targeted to improve your performance in The Body and Health Game.

Use the information in Part I of this book in the chapters "Time," "Structure," "Affinity," "Community," and "Purpose" to balance and coordinate The Body and Health Game with your overall Game plan.

✷ ✷ ✷

Congratulations, if you've chosen The Body and Health Game to restore and improve your health in 90 days. In the next chapter, you'll learn how to create and maintain a healthy bank account and turn your finances into positive resources instead of causes for worry and anxiety.

✷ ✷ ✷

★ Chapter 8 ★

Your Money

Playing The Game will help you make lifelong changes in how you relate to money. In this chapter, you'll get some of the most unusual financial advice you've ever heard.

But first, you have to transform your slave-and-beggar relationship with money into one in which you're satisfied with what you have while creating the capacity to get anything you want.

You've probably always thought of philanthropists as people who have vast sums of money and give it away to charities or the less fortunate. In an interview with *Modern Maturity's* reporter Claudia Dreifus (September–October 1999), Ted Turner says:

> In the first five years of my philanthropy, I gave away half of what I had. And that's a lot to give away when you're in your 50s. . . . As I learned to give more, I got more courageous. You have to be courageous to give. . . . It gives purpose to my life and makes me feel good to know that I'm at least trying to help out, that my money is a positive force in the world. Most of the happiest people I've met are generous people. Selfish people are usually pretty miserable.

I'm going to take Mr. Turner's philosophy of giving even further and share something with you that I've found to be true in my own life and in the lives of my coaching-program clients. When you begin designing your money budget by giving first to charities and churches, you're buying the kind of world you want to live in, the kind of planet you want to inhabit.

It probably sounds a little horrifying to think of giving or making donations first before spending money on anything else. How will you pay your living expenses or reduce your debt? Shouldn't you wait until "someday" or "later" when you're wealthy before you become a philanthropist?

Well, you already know my philosophy about waiting for someday and later. Whatever habits people have when they're less wealthy grow as their income increases. If you practice giving when you have very little, when you have a lot, you'll give more. Giving is a habit that makes you know emotionally and in every other way that you're wealthy enough to donate a portion of your income to others.

What if you start viewing yourself as a *giver* of money? A philanthropist, not in-the-making, but *now?* How powerful, free, and rich do you feel inside with that viewpoint? What if you automatically begin tithing and giving 10 percent to your church or donating to your favorite charities? How does this contrast with thinking of yourself as someone who earns a living, brings home a paycheck, or merely makes ends meet?

Through the simple reversal of giving to charities or churches first, you shift your relationship with money from something you're trying to *get* and are afraid of losing, to a resource that flows easily into your life. You've turned yourself into a conduit for money instead of being a bottleneck. This attitude and behavior leads to contentment and wealth. Becoming a giver balances your relationship with money, as giving and receiving become more equalized in your life. Because you're always finding opportunities for giving, there's a greater reason for you to receive a lot. You'll soon discover that it's impossible to out-give life.

A special rule for The Money Game is:
First, give a portion of your earnings
to charities and churches.

Giving and Returning

By clinging fearfully to money and hoarding it, the wealthy can live in poverty consciousness or scarcity mentality in the same way as poor individuals who are afraid to lose the little money they have. I'm suggesting that you break free of poverty consciousness by reprioritizing how you use money as a resource for yourself and others. Viewing money as limited keeps your resources small. An expansive view of yourself in relationship to money opens up vistas that you may have always thought were available only to the very rich and powerful. Nature abhors a vacuum. When you create one by giving a portion of your income away first, before using it for any other purpose, life refills and replenishes it in ways you could never have imagined.

The process of giving opens your heart and brings forth a joyful experience. When was the last time you gave in a way that set your heart aflutter and thrilled you? When did you give without a thought of expecting anything to return?

As you play The Money Game, you'll begin to transform your relationship with money by practicing the art of giving without expecting a return. This gift doesn't have to *be* money or even *cost* money. It can be an act of kindness or compassion. The act of giving puts you into The Game as a giver, a philanthropist, someone who isn't sitting on the sidelines, but who is a player—someone who makes a difference in the world.

A special rule for The Money Game is:
Each day, give something
without expecting anything in return.

Joyful Giving

There's a man (whom we'll call John Smith) in **TheCoach-ingProgram.com,** who, along with his wife (Mary) and daughter (Jane), uses the model of giving and saving first that I'm presenting in this book. Their story is an inspiration to all of us.

In the summer of 1978, after the sudden death of his brother, John underwent a profound spiritual change in his life. As he and Mary dealt with other challenges that year, they made a decision that would positively affect not only their own lives, but also the lives of many others. After deciding to let God take over their lives through the Holy Spirit, John was inspired to give more.

By December of 1978, John and Mary had given 10 percent of their earnings to their church. In January of 1979, John was shocked by the blessing of unprecedented business windfalls. It seemed to him that God was acknowledging and encouraging the changes their family had made with respect to giving *first*. For three years in a row, the family's tithing was followed by extraordinarily profitable business in January.

Because John and Mary Smith so enjoyed giving, they began to make an enterprise of philanthropy. In addition to tithing, until the mid-'80s, the family contributed annually to more than 100 different charities. Today they've narrowed down their list of charities to the manageable number of 20. In addition, every year since 1978, the couple has increased the percentage of their income that they give. By the year 2001, they intend to donate approximately one-third of their available income to charity!

At first, the Smiths were making their donations at the end of the year. But then they decided that they didn't want to play catch-up in December to achieve their donation goals, so they started the practice of giving in advance of earning their income. At the beginning of each month, they made their charitable donations. Now, they often give heavily at the start of each year—sometimes, for tax reasons, even the preceding December—and trust that God will provide the income to take care of their own needs.

John says that this type of giving is their own covenant with God, a way of showing appreciation for all their gifts and blessings. In the 22 years since they've been engaging in philanthropy, despite economic and health setbacks, the Smiths have only experienced a downdraft in their net worth for one year. They view what they do as honoring God by channeling the assets under their control back into their community.

The Smiths give out of love to organizations, which are in alignment with their higher purpose, and to charities doing work the family cares deeply about. Because of their strong religious faith, the family predominantly supports churches, ministries, and other charities for which Mary also volunteers her time and services. John calls what they do "joyful giving."

Systematic Giving and Receiving

John didn't grow up or start off his business career as a wealthy man, but from the start of their marriage, the Smiths shared the philosophy that personal debt is the opposite of giving. They consider debt to be a selfish act that keeps a person from being in a position to give to others. Consequently, the Smiths always saved until they could afford to buy what they wanted, and they managed to pay cash for the purchase of their first and second homes. Because they never pay interest, John says, "Our first fruits go back to God and not to a banker or lender. God has always provided for us, so we can cheerfully give to charities."

John and Mary are raising their daughter, Jane, with their same money values. They divide the 13-year-old's allowance the way they've portioned out their own income, using the method described on the next page. John says, "Using this discipline will make anyone financially independent in ten years," and, as a financial services advisor, he recommends it to his clients.

So here are some secrets to John's financial success. First, he encourages apportioning and prioritizing the family's earned income in the following ways:

- 5 percent for the poor or less fortunate
- 10 percent for the church
- 15 percent into long-term savings and investments, without ever touching the money again but with the understanding that it's okay to spend or reinvest earned interest or dividends
- 20 percent for short-term savings or deferred consumption to use for buying items such as appliances, insurance, gifts, or luxury items
- 50 percent for living expenses.

Jane Smith says, "Sometimes, I wish I had *more* than 50 percent of my allowance to spend, but I really like the fact that I'm saving up for a car I can buy when I get older."

Jane says she enjoys the wonderful feelings she has when she can buy a soft drink or give a gift to a friend who is less fortunate than she is. When she was eight years old, Jane liked being able to personally donate the portion she'd saved from her allowance (an envelope with eight dollars in it) to a church that regularly feeds the poor. John says that his daughter, growing up with the kind of money values he and his wife model, has become a natural giver. The couple often marvels at how generous she is.

In addition to the division of income he employs, John also practices five rules he gladly shares with others:

1. *Remember that you're a steward, not an owner.* You only possess things while you're alive, and these possessions are entrusted to you.

2. *Spend less than you earn.*

3. *Avoid debt.* It's the antithesis of giving. Do not borrow money for consumption items.

4. *Save a little regularly, every month, every week.*

5. *Have a financial plan.*

John says, "We love to give. We don't let ourselves be taken advantage of, and we won't be used. But we love to give."

Perhaps you'd like to add the Smith family's guidelines for apportioning income to your Money Game. It can't hurt you, but it sure could help.

Savings and Investments

Do you tell yourself that you'll save and invest money when you have some to spend? That you'll do it when your rent or house payment and bills are paid? Or when you've lowered or ended your credit-card debt?

To play The Money Game, I'm suggesting that, like John and his family do, after making a donation to a charity or church, you put a portion of your income into savings or investments *before* you do anything else with it. When you devote money to savings and investments before spending it, you're creating the opportunity for more money to come back to you. Saving and investing first means that you (an *A Relationship*) are *taking care* of you (an *A Activity*).

There's very little satisfaction in spending all your money on living expenses. Instead of following your dreams, you're chasing an ever-accelerating cycle of keeping up with how much everyone around you is spending on shiny, new toys. These kind of spending habits produce unnecessary stress. When you devote money exclusively to living expenses and luxury items, you're more dissatisfied, because the desire to increase consumption is insatiable. You'll always find new ways to spend money no matter how much your income increases. When you save and invest *first*, you'll be more inclined to use the money that's left over for needs instead of desires. And you'll have the comfort of knowing that a portion of your income is growing in a savings account or some other sort of investment.

If you use the bulk of your earnings on living expenses, you create the consciousness in yourself of someone who is only here on this earth to earn a living. This causes you to ignore the fact that you have a higher purpose, and money is a resource for helping fulfill it.

A special rule for The Money Game is:
Save or invest before spending.

Where to Give?

Okay, let's say you're now convinced that giving away a portion of your income first, before you pay bills or buy more "stuff," is a priority. How will you know whom or what to give your money to? Aren't there thousands of worthy causes? Millions of needy hands extended?

At this point, you need to refer back to the chapter and section of your Game journal where you began formulating the statement of your higher purpose. Align giving with your higher purpose and what is most important to you. This makes the decision of where to give money very simple.

Also, remember to start your charitable giving by putting money back into the local community, because this increases the prosperity of your very own environment. Many local organizations are really structures set up to facilitate giving. By supporting your community charities, you're helping to fulfill your purpose and theirs.

A special rule for The Money Game is:
Align giving with your higher purpose.

Money and Spending Priorities

To recap the order for prioritizing how to use money as a resource in The Money Game, refer to the figure below.

The Money Game

#1   Giving/Tithing
#2   Savings
#3   Investment
#4   Community
#5   Living Expenses

A special rule for The Money Game is:
Reprioritize your spending in the following order: giving to charities and churches, saving, investing, giving to your local community, and paying living expenses.

Changing Your Relationship to Daily Living Expenses

Most people have a great desire for money, and there's nothing wrong with that. The problem arises when the desire for money becomes so important that they're constantly fretting over whether they have a lot or a little. They've become imbalanced over the issue of money.

You've probably noticed that as your income has increased, so have your appetites. This is why you find yourself in the same financial position no matter how much money you make. Playing The Money Game will help you develop balance. To do so, you'll have to observe how you're currently spending money.

When I played The Money Game, I noticed that I'd been spending an extraordinary amount of money eating in restaurants. The only thing more obscene than the money I was dropping into the local economy was how much weight I was gaining by not carefully preparing my own food at home.

I decided to take the same amount of money I was spending on restaurant food, eat at home, and dedicate the money I was saving to hiring an excellent physical fitness instructor and a wonderful yoga teacher. With those same dollars, I bought an opportunity to restore my body back to health. This also created a balance that spread throughout my entire life.

By observing where you're currently spending money, you'll see whether or not you're placing it in alignment with your higher purpose and if you're spending money in the areas of life you find satisfying or that need the most improvement.

Keep a seven-day log of exactly how you're spending every penny. Analyze your spending by categorizing items such as eating in restaurants; and paying for movies, videos, books, magazines, clothing, food, utilities, health services, credit card bills, and charitable contributions. Make this log as personal and detailed as possible so it communicates exactly where your money is currently going.

Use this financial log to make decisions about which categories you need to modify in order to accomplish your Money Game goals, as well as improving the other areas of life you've selected in your 90-day Game.

A special rule for The Money Game is:
*Keep a seven-day financial log,
and analyze how you're spending money.*

Owned by Possessions and Debt

Most people drain their resources by engaging in escapist activities. Their lives aren't really working for them, so they compensate by *buying* things. How often do you see a sports car, which is small and beautiful, being driven by an ego that's large and distorted? There's nothing wrong with purchasing what you want as long as you're not clinging to the illusion that these items are necessary for your happiness. When people say, "I own this," in truth they might as well be saying, "This possession owns me." Being owned by your possessions is how you become a slave to money. Once you decide to be satisfied with what you have, it's a lot easier to create much more.

You might think that paying the rent or credit-card bills first shows that you're taking care of yourself. When you pay your debt first, before giving or saving, you stay stuck in an ever-increasing cycle of debt because the tendency is to accumulate more debt as you think of more things to buy. All you're doing is treading in quicksand. Paying off debt alone is never going to get you anywhere.

If you take a look at how you've created the debt, you'll notice that it's developed—not by taking care of living expenses, but from buying luxury items. There's nothing wrong with luxury unless it becomes a measure of enjoyment in your life. When you satisfy yourself emotionally through luxury purchases, this is when there seems to be no end to the amount of debt you can pile on yourself.

Some people cut up their credit cards, but they haven't cut up their habit of acquiring, so they've changed nothing. In The Money Game, you'll change your fundamental thinking about money, as opposed to making changes in how much money you have or don't have. By instituting structures to help yourself feel balanced and content about money, you'll have the flexibility to relate to money in a whole new way.

A special rule for The Money Game is:
Analyze how to positively change your relationship to
money, possessions, and debt.

The Money Game's Coaches

You definitely want to get good coaching to help you design The Money Game. You'll be looking for coaches who can help you do financial planning, do budgeting for daily expenses, and decide how to fulfill The Money Game goals of local philanthropy, savings, and investments. There are so many solid, reasonable, and practical approaches to money management. You'll have to choose what appeals to you, what will keep you motivated, and what aligns with your higher purpose.

I've been in the financial services industry for most of my professional career. Over the years, I've met some terrific financial management coaches. On the **TheGameInteractive.com** Website, you can click onto "The Money Game" and read profiles of some of the outstanding financial service coaches whom I've certified as knowledgeable in The Game's technology.

Don't overlook the obvious when planning The Money Game. Almost any bank will show you how to balance your checkbook. Libraries are filled with books and literature on financial planning. Financial services companies offer free seminars, lectures, and initial consultations. Coaching resources abound for helping you deliver on the commitment to improve your money situation in 90 days. The key to winning a healthy money life is to take action instead of just thinking or complaining about the dire shape you're in.

A special rule for The Money Game is:
Get financial coaches and have a plan.

MONEY GAME EXERCISE

Use activities that feature the special rules above if you decide to make The Money Game one of the three to five aspects of life you want to improve in 90 days. Also, design The Money Game by using The Game's basic elements described in Part III of this book: goals, To-Be and Not-To-Be lists, points, prizes, rules, Before-and-After Displays, essays, skills, rewards, consequences, deadlines, partners, and coaches.

✳ ✳ ✳

If you're adopting a financial planning or management system for The Money Game, give yourself points for using it. An example of a consequence for not achieving your goals in The Money Game could be that if you don't save the amount each week that you said you would, you'll carry a tin cup around *everywhere* for three days and ask *everyone,* including total strangers, to contribute to your savings account because you didn't put enough money in it. Refer to **TheGameInteractive.com** Website for more ideas and coaching specifically targeted to improving your performance in The Money Game.

Use the information in Part I of this book in the chapters "Time," "Structure," "Affinity," "Community," and "Purpose" to balance and coordinate The Money Game with your overall Game plan.

Congratulations! You've taken the first step in winning your financial health in 90 days. In the next chapter, you'll learn techniques for improving all of the relationships in your life.

★ ★ ★

★ CHAPTER 9 ★

Your Relationships

You might be wondering how something as serious as your relationships could be improved by playing The Game. If you choose this aspect of life as an area you want to focus on for 90 days, you'll be delighted to discover that relighting the flame of a relationship is a lot easier when you make it fun and creative. Criticizing and finding fault with people causes tension and withdrawal. Making relationship repair an aspect of The Game brings about joy and compassion.

You'll learn in The Relationship Game that even if you've been a failure at intimacy or friendship in the past, you can now become proficient at these important elements of living a full and meaningful life.

Relationships don't usually turn sour suddenly. Their fractures are detectable long before a final breakup occurs. Playing The Relationship Game will help you detect where things are unraveling in your most important relationships and give you the structure and support for dealing with issues now, instead of "later" or "someday."

Relationship Coaching

If you decide that you want to focus on improving your ability to have satisfying relationships as an aspect of your Game, you're going to do more than analyze your relationships. You'll be taking action that requires courage and honesty. As part of The Relationship Game, you'll interview the people around you and ask them about the quality of your relationships with them. You'll pose two very simple but powerful questions:

1. What do you like most about our relationship?
2. How can I improve our relationship?

Instead of getting defensive or argumentative, you're going to listen intently to the answers your spouse, friends, family members, co-workers, and associates give to those two questions. Then, you'll design The Relationship Game to change behaviors, attitudes, and habits that they've told you would improve relationships with them.

It's So Simple

In 90 days, by using The Game's technology, you'll transform weak, tottering-on-the-brink-of-disaster relationships into strong and healthy ones.

Sound simple?

It is. But asking the two questions above and sincerely listening to and accepting the answers without argument may be one of the toughest yet most valuable things you've ever done for yourself and the people you care about.

Sally Vail, a Game-player in our coaching program, tells what happened when one of our master instructors, Dr. Martin Kettelhut (we call him "Doc"), advised Sally to ask the two relationship questions of a VIP in her life.

Sally writes:

I knew that I wanted a major breakthrough in the area of relationships with men in general, particularly with my father. Doc, my brilliant coach, gave me my first relationship assignment for The Game. He instructed me to drive to Connecticut, where my father lives, and ask him two questions: What do you like most about me? *and* How can I improve our relationship?

Well, considering the fact that I visit my father only once a year, and our conversations are mainly about the weather, I was a little intimidated by the thought of probing so deeply into our relationship. But I knew that the father-thing and the relating-to-men-thing are, of course, directly related to each other. So I accepted my first coaching assignment— VERY RELUCTANTLY. As I was driving, I cried, because I realized that at 37 years of age, I was still walking around thinking that my father doesn't LIKE ME!

My father and I met for lunch. I was grateful that we were outdoors so I could wear sunglasses, and he wouldn't see that I'd been crying. But as I tried to ask the first question, the tears started streaming down my face. I don't know what he thought I was attempting to say, but by the time I could speak, he was probably relieved that I didn't reveal some terrible truth or tragedy.

After I managed to ask the questions, my father started to answer me as I thought he would, by saying, "What do you mean? You're my daughter. I love you."

Through my tears, I said, "That's not what I asked. I want to know what you like about me."

To my surprise, my father listed about 20 different things that he liked about me. These were qualities about myself that I didn't have a clue he'd ever noticed. He told me that he liked the fact that I was ethical in what could be an unethical business. He liked my values, my sense of humor, and my strong will.

I was blown away, because I didn't even think he liked me at all!

Then I asked, "Okay, what do you think I need to improve?"

He said, "Nothing."

I said. "Nothing?"

Then he told me, "Well, you used to have to fix everyone in the family, but you don't do that anymore."

After this opening, we continued to talk for hours. My father told me about his childhood, his relationship with his parents, and how he felt about his life. I can honestly say that I never really knew this man before that afternoon.

As I drove back home, I was now crying tears of joy. I felt so grateful for the precious time I'd just spent with my dad. If something happens to him, I feel such a sense of relief that I'm really complete with our relationship. Having lunch with him that day and asking those two questions changed our relationship forever.

A special rule for The Relationship Game is:
Ask important people in your life: **"What do you like about me?"** *and* **"How can I improve our relationship?"**

Look for Themes

As you ask the two relationship questions of the people around you, look for themes in their answers. These common threads are items you can put on your Relationship Game To-Be and Not-To-Be lists. When one of my coaching clients asked his associates, friends, and family members what he could improve in his relationships with them, they consistently told him that he talked too much. Of course, all his life, everyone knew this about him. But until then, nobody had ever told him—

probably because he'd never given them the opportunity to.

After the man had these conversations, he started asking people to tell him when he was talking too much, and added the skill of saying things more briefly and succinctly as a goal on his To-Be list. This client was using feedback he received to improve his ability to relate to others by leaps and bounds. Others could now trust that they'd be able to express their own thoughts and ideas to him, and that conversation with him wouldn't take up too much of their time.

A special rule for The Relationship Game is:
Whatever needs improvement in your relationship
with others can be added to your Game.

Lining Up Your Good Intentions with Your Behavior

In The Relationship Game, you're likely to discover that your single greatest blind spot is yourself. You have intentions, which only you know, but often your behavior doesn't line up with them. When you ask people the two questions, you'll be able to immediately see aspects of relationships where you aren't communicating your good intentions. For example, you may deeply love someone, but your actions don't show it. While playing The Relationship Game for 90 days, you'll have the opportunity to establish behaviors and habits that convey how you really feel about the people you love.

For 67 consecutive days, newlywed George Thompson bought his wife a gift and delivered it to her at work. Because he had to be at his office earlier than she did, George would drop off the gift-of-the-day to the security guard in his wife's building and ask him to deliver it to her when she arrived.

George says that because he was giving his wife so many gifts, he set a budget for himself of having the presents each cost five dollars or less. This meant that he became creative in giving her items that would express his love without cost-ing a lot of money. On his lunch hour, he'd pick up trinkets such as candies, little toys or gadgets that would bring a smile to his wife's face, or special items to which he could attach love notes. Sometimes he just wrote his sentiments in a letter and put it in an envelope with a bow on top.

At first, his wife's office mates were amused by the young husband's ardor. However, as the gifts continued, they started getting a little envious. Then, things changed again, and some-thing wonderful happened. People started passing by George's wife's desk and smiling at the plethora of mementos expressing her husband's affection. Since smiles have a way of becoming infectious, the atmosphere in his wife's entire office became lighter and more loving.

George says that one of his greatest pleasures, in addition to his wife's gratitude for having such an affectionate husband, was that when Valentine's Day came that year, other women were getting their one token of love from husbands and boyfriends while his wife's desk was piled high with over two months' worth of appreciation. A co-worker commented, "Every day is Valentine's Day for you!"

George found a wonderfully creative way to line up his feel-ings and good intentions with a habit that he instituted in his Relationship Game. Other Game-players have also found cre-ative ways to express their feelings:

- Dean Lampe made a commitment to tell his wife and son at least once each day that he loves them. But he wanted this to be more than a mechanical reflex, so he always gave them a reason *why* he loved them. And each reason had to be different. Consequently, Dean's family members heard 90 unique reasons why he loved them.

- Greg Kadet made it part of his Relationship Game to talk less and listen more. He said that for 90 days, whenever he went out with people, he curbed his tendency to take control of conversations. He was often amused by how often people would end their visits with him by saying what a great time they'd had.

- Tom Batson says that while playing The Relationship Game, "my listening skills went from mono to hi-fi."

- Mary Wichmann gave herself points in The Relationship Game for doing romantic things such as giving her husband a neck massage as they drove home together from work or smooching with him when they were alone on an elevator. She actively looked for ways to show her husband how special he was to her. Sometimes, when Mary provided him with extra attention, he'd remind her to give herself points for those gestures of affection.

- Grover Stults says that his wife, Pam, really enjoys the fact that playing The Relationship Game inspired him to make their bed every morning and to drive closer to the speed limit.

A special rule for The Relationship Game is:
Show and express your good intentions
and true, loving feelings.

Time for Those Long Talks

During your Relationship Game, it's time to have those long talks you've been avoiding and putting off for "sometime" or "later." You know which people this refers to. These are the ones with whom you have unfinished business. They're the relationships that ended badly or fizzled out from lack of attention.

These are the people with whom you've had misunderstandings and miscommunications. These are the long talks where you're going to forgive and be forgiven. They're the tough ones. You've probably been dreading them. But now you're going to apologize, make amends, take responsibility, and clean up messes.

We're going back to Sally Vail, who practically became a relationship master when she played The Game in our coaching program. Her experience can inspire all of us to take that extra step with painful relationships.

Sally says:

> *While I played The Game, I was very committed to improving my health and getting into great shape. My mother is an alcoholic who has been drinking my entire life. While I played The Game, she was staying at my house, trying to figure out where she wanted to live. One afternoon when we were talking, I decided to have a serious conversation with her. I told my mother that if she didn't stop drinking, I was sure our relationship would get worse. If she did stop, I guaranteed it would get better.*
>
> *I've said things like this to my mother, but something was different this time. I WAS DIFFERENT. I wasn't interested in rescuing her or telling her what to do. For the first time in my life, I was committed to myself, my health, and my well-being. I wasn't running around trying to fix things outside of myself, but was focused on taking responsibility for my own life.*
>
> *Well, a miracle occurred about three weeks after we had that conversation. My mother entered Alcoholics Anonymous! This woman HAS NEVER tried to quit drinking before in her life! As of this October 31st, she's been sober, healthy, and*

honest for one year. Our relationship has never been more fulfilling. She's this incredible, vibrant, amazing lady who now knows and honors herself.

I attribute this change in her to my example of how to live life to the fullest while I played The Game. What I was doing for myself inspired her to change her own life!

Notice that the change in Sally's mother didn't happen as a result of Sally delivering a lecture or harangue. Instead, Sally, as a true leader, inspired someone else by her example. This may be one of the most difficult ways to heal relationships rather than trying to fix them. It's only natural, when you make gargantuan efforts to repair relationships, that you'd expect to be met part or halfway. That's not the focus of your Relationship Game, though. Your Game, as in Sally's case, is to handle yourself, offer those olive branches everywhere you can, and stay detached from the outcomes.

A special double-sided rule for The Relationship Game is:
Have those long talks you've been putting off; make amends for hurts or wrongs you've caused.

Where Are You When You're Upset?

Those long-held hurts and feelings of guilt are the emotions that have led to your need to make amends. Emotions play a large part in the building or breaking down of relationships. Think about the range of emotions you might feel in a day—anger, surprise, joy, guilt, anxiety, and more. Each emotion has a relationship to time. Guilt is an emotion of the past; you're guilty and regret something you've previously said or done. Anxiety is an emotion of the future; you're anxious over what might happen. Love, in its purest form, is an emotion of the present. If you put love in the past, it becomes something you're missing and turns into regret. If you put love into the future, it turns into longing and pining. The emotion of love can really only exist in the present. This is also true for the emotions of peace, contentment, reverence, and joy.

Take a look at the chart below as a reference point for how to catch yourself in time when you're feeling emotional.

Time	Associated Emotion
The Past	Guilt, jealousy, anger, misery, depression, resentment
The Future	Anxiety, worry, panic, greed, fear
The Present	Love, happiness, contentment, peacefulness, joy, reverence, gratitude

Which emotions would you rather be consistently feeling? Would you prefer being joyful and content or angry and anxious?

Game-player Steve Powilatis shares how he's learned to identify and express what he's feeling in the moment to create healthier relationships.

Steve says:

Dealing with my emotions has allowed me to bring them into the present instead of keeping my emotions locked up inside. During The Game, I stopped putting on the face of being supercompetent. I began to express whatever I was feeling in the present. This allowed emotions to dissolve. Even if it was just a matter of getting things off my chest, the ability to say what I'm feeling helped me become more authentic and not feel the need to be good at everything. I became truer to myself. I wasn't judging my emotions as being right or wrong, just true for me. Changing how I handled my emotions helped me become clearer and more honest with my co-workers, friends, and family.

Steve has shown the wisdom of what I'm going to share with you as a basic key for dealing with your emotions successfully.

A special rule for The Relationships Game is:
Recognize when an emotion is in the past or future, and quickly bring yourself into the present.

Play It Again Sam, Only Faster

If you're like most people, you have conversations in your mind about whatever you consider to be the source of your unhappiness in relationships. You can relieve yourself of mentally splashing in mud puddles by doubling your pace. This isn't the same as becoming frantic or being driven into action because you're uncertain. Instead, you're moving with velocity rather than the erratic movements people use when they're feeling fearful.

When you deliberately double your pace, you'll unconsciously move out of the slow pace where suffering and upsetting emotions are controlling you. The velocity will cause you to place your full attention on whatever you're doing right now. This frees your mind to experience emotions that occur in the present, such as joy and contentment.

Moving slowly through your day and activities allows your mind to daydream and to give attention to all the things about your life and others that upset you and keep you anxious. Doubling your pace allows you to connect with what's in front of you right now and experience peacefulness in the present moment. When you pick up your pace, you're operating at a level of efficiency that is very different from plodding along, allowing your unconscious mind to intervene to remind you how miserable you are.

A special rule for The Relationships Game is:
When you feel upset or emotional, rather than taking your emotions out on others, double the pace of whatever you're doing.

The Relationship Blame Game

Look at the relationships you're in right now. Think about all the things you don't like, and the ways in which you'd like the other person to change. You're probably thinking that if the other person *does* change those things, the relationship will improve, right? In relationships where people take no responsibility, they're usually much clearer about what someone *else* should be doing and unclear about the behaviors they themselves need to change.

When I take a look at my life, I see a classic example of someone who spent the early part of it involved in blame, judgment, and not taking responsibility for himself. It was very easy for me to say, "You know, I'd have more opportunities if I weren't black." What a perfect set of beliefs to keep me in a prison of my own making!

I entered college at the age of 16, and was intellectually, but not emotionally, prepared for the freedom of college life. To avoid taking responsibility for myself, I became very clear that if only I had as much money as other kids, my grades would be better. If I'd gone to the kind of high schools they did, college would be easier for me. If the other students would let me belong to their crowd, I'd be able to focus more. In other words, I became a classic whiner and blamer.

Fortunately, I grew out of this tendency to blame others and not take responsibility for my own life and actions. I asked myself: *True or not, how does viewing myself as a victim change my condition in any way?* I concluded that if I'm a victim, here's the bad news—basically, I'm stuck. I've lost my freedom through victimhood. I might have the feeling that I'm right, I might get to blame others for my problems, and I'd get to judge them. What I wouldn't get is the life I wanted.

When my ex-wife and I were divorcing, my daughter, Georgia (who was then six), and I went for a walk one day. She asked me, "What did I do wrong, Daddy, that made you and Mommy break up?" Of course I reassured her that the divorce wasn't her fault. Later, I talked to a therapist about Georgia's question. She told me that children often take on responsibility for their family's lives and blame themselves personally for divorce. By contrast, we adults often don't take on *enough* responsibility for what's going on in our relationships. Instead, we place the burden on others—even on the world at large. We also blame everything that went on in our childhoods. What a setup!

A special rule for The Relationship Game is:
*Stop blaming others, and take responsibility
for how your life is turning out.*

The Relationship's Higher Purpose

Finally, in The Relationship Game, you want to be sure that you and your partner, family member, or friend are aligning behind the higher purpose of the relationship. When you talk with people who mean a lot to you, share what you believe your higher purpose to be. Then discuss what the higher purpose of the two of you together might be.

One couple I know have established a charitable foundation to share, distribute, and publish stories that help people gain a deeper understanding of the gifts and blessings animals provide. They say that one of the shared higher purposes of their relationship is to increase love and respect for all life. Each time, before this husband and wife do their public presentations, they sit together, hold hands, and remind themselves that they are "a golden team, dedicated to giving service to all life."

When you design and articulate a higher purpose for your relationship, it's easier to align all you do and say behind it. This focus enables you to select any books, audiocassettes, programs, or relationship seminars that truly align with your higher purpose.

A special rule for The Relationship Game is:
Explore the shared higher purpose of your relationships.

RELATIONSHIP GAME EXERCISES

Do the exercises that follow if you decide to make The Relationship Game one of the three to five aspects of life you want to improve in 90 days. Also, design The Relationship Game by using The Game's basic elements described in Part III of this book: goals, To-Be and Not-To-Be lists, points, prizes, rules, Before-and-After Displays, essays, skills, rewards, consequences, deadlines, partners, and coaches.

If you're adopting a special therapy or system for The Relationship Game, give yourself points for using it. An example of a consequence for not achieving goals in The Relationship Game is when one gentleman, who has a beautiful head of hair, said that he'd shave himself bald if he didn't keep his relationship commitments. Refer to **TheGameInteractive.com** Website for more ideas and coaching specifically targeted to improving your performance in The Relationship Game.

Use the information in Part I of this book in the chapters "Time," "Structure," "Affinity," "Community," and "Purpose" to balance and coordinate The Relationship Game with your overall Game plan.

EXERCISE: THE BLAME GAME

Examine your personal life, neighborhood, work, business, and the planet, and list whatever you believe other people should be doing but are not. Start each sentence with the words: *"People"*. . . or *"They should"*. . . and fill in the blanks. Next, write the names of people who join you in playing "The Blame Game." Last, look for patterns in the individuals or types of people you tend to most often blame.

Now, replace the words *People* or *They* with *I*. Rewrite your list with the words: *I should* . . .

This is how you can stop playing The Blame Game and start playing . . . The Game. You can also use this exercise to identify people who support your habit of blaming and whining. Notice who you're regularly handing your freedom and power to through the process of blame.

✳ ✳ ✳

In the next chapter, you'll see how to increase your spiritual growth and peace of mind no matter what your religious beliefs (or non-beliefs) might be.

✳ ✳ ✳

✶ CHAPTER 10 ✶

Your Spiritual Life

You've probably heard the old adage that life is a journey, not a destination. The same could be said for playing The Spiritual Life Game. It is a journey toward self-discovery, deeper meaning; or a connection with God, the Sacred, the Divine, or whatever you relate to as a power or force greater, vaster, and wiser than yourself. If you've been absorbed in fulfilling your daily duties and responsibilities, striving to make more money, struggling to stay ahead, or talking much more than you listen, playing The Spiritual Life Game will restore balance, sanity, dignity, and meaning to your existence.

During these 90 days, you'll make a priority out of nourishing your spirit and reflecting on the underlying purpose of your life. In the next three months, you can reach a higher level of spiritual development and discover what lessons life has been teaching you.

I've had the honor and pleasure of coaching and working with some of the wealthiest people on the planet. I've often noticed that when people haven't developed a spiritual core, they increasingly gather material goods, yet their lives become more unstable and insecure. In The Spiritual Life Game, you'll be learning how to simultaneously be content with what you have, while expanding your ability to accomplish anything you want. This puts you in a position to make money and actually enjoy it. And when your life is characterized by a deeper meaning at its core, money can serve the purpose of furthering your spiritual development. For example, money can afford you the opportunity to attend spiritual retreats and seminars, support endeavors that are oriented toward this area of life, or feed your spirit in any number of ways.

If you're an agnostic or atheist, you can play The Spiritual Life Game by focusing on the fulfillment of your purpose as a human being. Your Game can revolve around helping all of humanity through volunteerism, charitable acts, or just being a compassionate person who serves as a model for your fellow human beings. All of these acts comprise elements of spirituality that aren't necessarily connected to a belief in God or a Higher Power.

As with each of the other Games on the playing field you design, you can plug in whatever principles, beliefs, or goals you feel would improve your life in that area. Then, use The Game's technology to achieve them. I really don't care *what* you believe. I only encourage you to explore, practice, and deepen whatever it is that brings you joy and fulfillment.

Now or Later

Many people don't think about their spiritual lives until they're faced with a crisis such as a life-threatening illness. Then they decide to embark on spiritual practices such as meditation or prayer.

Are you ready to turn "later" and "someday" into "now" when it comes to attending to your spiritual life? I have some questions for you to consider if spirituality has been so far back on your burner that you've forgotten that it's an essential part of being human:

- Why would you wait until you're about to die to focus on spirituality, when it could be enriching absolutely everything in your life today?

- How much more prepared for dealing with life's greatest challenges (including death) will you be if you make a commitment right now to nourish your spirit in whatever way works best for you?

- How long are you going to keep depriving yourself of that which will bring you more satisfaction than anything the material world has to offer?

Try this exercise: Pretend you're going to die within 24 hours. What is most important to you: watching a sunset or sunrise, reading the Bible or some other literature that gives you strength or perspective, communing with nature, playing with your children . . . ? Whatever it is, if it's good enough for you when you're dying, then it should certainly be important enough to pay attention to while you're alive.

Think about those times when people close to you were dying. What did they request at the end of their lives? Did they want to be near family members or personal mementos? Did they crave good, honest, heartfelt conversation? These are the kinds of things you want in your life, which will nourish you every day.

A special rule for The Spiritual Life Game is:
Live each day as if it were your last.

Exploring What You Believe

When the subject of spirituality comes up in conversation, people often admit that they don't know what they believe. They have no idea what speaks to their hearts. This can be a result of *spiritual immaturity.* By this term, I mean that people are often still in a reactive or rebellious mode when it comes to their spiritual lives.

Perhaps long ago they rejected their parents' religion or the kind of belief system that they felt was foisted upon them as children. Yet they haven't taken the time or made the effort to seek out something that is more to their liking. These individuals are still mired in teenage rebellion or an ego-driven mode where they're too proud to even consider that their parents might have been wise about anything. These attitudes may be robbing them of possibilities for spiritual growth.

This doesn't mean that because you've rejected that old-time religion, you are wrong and your parents were right. What it does mean is that if you've never explored your childhood belief system for yourself, you could be stuck in a knee-jerk reaction to your parents' authority rather than having made up your own mind about the religious traditions with which you were raised.

Or, perhaps the opposite form of spiritual immaturity may be true for you. If you've merely accepted whatever has been handed down to you by your parents without ever exploring its deeper meaning, you haven't allowed for the possibility that this tradition might satisfy you in ways that your parents could have never imagined.

These are the kinds of issues you'll want to consider as you design The Spiritual Life Game. What's truly *yours*, and what have you merely accepted or rejected? What would offer you a more satisfying and meaningful spiritual life than you had as a child? Or what would restore the innocence and joy you may have found in your spiritual life back then?

A special rule for The Spiritual Life Game is:
Develop a sense of maturity in your
spiritual beliefs and practices.

Living Versus Talking

To wholeheartedly play The Spiritual Life Game, I suggest that you do more than just talk about religion, beliefs, or traditions. Find the structure and community that will help you start living what you say you believe. If you're a church member, talk with the minister and ask how you can become more involved in this place of worship. If going to church doesn't fit in with how you want to feed your spiritual life, take regular walks with your friends in the woods, and worship together there. The point is to surround yourself with people who have an affinity for expressing and developing their spirituality.

George Page shares a story of how he found comfort and growth in a spiritual community.

He says:

When I was 69 years old, I had to undergo surgery to remove a malignant prostate gland. I was a bit anxious to get it done as quickly as possible before aggressive cancer cells spread.

While driving to a vacation spot where I'd be spending a week with my family, I started wondering what I was supposed to be learning from this totally unexpected experience of having cancer surgery. The answer that came to mind was: Since no one really knows exactly what causes this or other cancers, I should change my life in as many ways as possible.

I decided to institute changes by starting with acting as if I were a Catholic and joining my wife by going to church with her. This was something I hadn't done for more than 40 years.

The next day after my decision, we attended Mass at a Catholic church. There, I received amazing validation that I was doing the right thing. We were welcomed into the church with the sound of fantastic organ music. I felt as if we were attending a concert. An old Irish priest officiated the service and held out his open arms to people of all beliefs, telling them to "do their own thing." His attitude made me feel immediately comfortable.

My surgery and the recovery from it turned out to be totally successful. Since then, I've continued to go to Mass when I wanted this kind of spiritual connection, and I feel that I'm on a journey to raise my life to a higher level.

By making the change of revisiting his old spiritual beliefs, George had the kind of renewal he was seeking.

You may have been caught up in the form or the organization of having a spiritual life and lost its true substance. If you're honest with yourself, you may realize that you're more charged up by the power and attention that comes from talking about your religious beliefs and getting others interested in them than living your religion and leading by example.

Perhaps you're someone who volunteers in your church and busily manages all sorts of activities, yet when it comes to your own prayer life, you run out of time. Maybe you're giving much, but with a lot of fanfare and praise. You may have lost the ability not to expect anything in return from doing silent and compassionate acts. Or are you someone who lives by the *letter* but not the *spirit* of the law? These are points to reflect upon as you decide what your Spiritual Life Game should consist of for 90 days.

Before going to bed and upon waking up, imagine what your day would look like if you lived it according to your highest principles and beliefs. For example, you might practice not judging others. When you see someone you'd normally internally criticize, instead of judging, just say a hearty "Good morning," and welcome the person with love in your heart.

A special rule for The Spiritual Life Game is:
Live what you believe.

Spiritual Practices for Beginning and Ending Your Day

In previous chapters, I've discussed that a general rule of The Game is to spend a majority of your time engaging in *A Activities* with *A Relationships.* I mentioned that spending time with yourself is an *A Relationship.* Spiritual practice is a way of having an *A Activity* with an *A Relationship* (you or others who join you in this spiritual practice).

There are three spiritual practices I'm suggesting that you do when you play The Spiritual Life Game. Perhaps you're already incorporating these practices, but for your Spiritual Life Game, you'll want to do them more consistently or frequently for 90 days.

They are:

1. *Engage in a spiritual observance of your own choosing for a minimum of ten minutes in the morning and at least five minutes before you go to sleep at night.* This can be the practice of prayer, meditation, contemplation, singing songs or hymns, performing a sacred ritual, or whatever allows you to connect spiritually with your heart and your beliefs. I also encourage you to do spiritual practices often throughout your day. Ed Dawson, a coaching client, played The Spiritual Life Game and scheduled exactly when, where, and with whom he would meditate each day. Then he gave himself points for keeping these commitments to his spiritual growth.

2. *Before bedtime, put your thoughts and emotions to rest and give thanks for the day.* Game-player Miguel Sosa finds that evening reflection and quiet time leads to a better life and a good night's sleep.

Miguel says:

For many years, I've lived with restless sleep and poor digestion. Since playing The Game, I've started taking a moment to set my mind at ease at night and gain control of my thoughts. I put my insecurities and anxieties to rest.

I'm realizing that I've been using an enormous amount of energy throughout the day in fighting my thoughts and rationalizing my actions. Since starting the practice of stilling my thoughts and emotions before going to bed, I'm sleeping better, and my digestion has improved. I wake up feeling rested because I haven't spent the night wrestling with my emotions and insecurities.

3. *Read and reflect on spiritual literature that is meaningful to you, especially in the morning,* so you can start your day with inspiration. Do the same at night so you can have a restful night's sleep with pleasant dreams. You might also memorize spiritual quotes or devise affirmations that you repeat during the day to enrich this practice.

Refresh

What do you think of when you hear that something is refreshing or has been refreshed? When I looked up the word *refresh* in the thesaurus, it offered the synonyms: *enliven, invigorate, rejuvenate, energize, restore, pep up, recharge,* and *revitalize.* It said that the opposite of *refresh* is to "wear out."

The spiritual practice you'll be engaging in during The Game—especially in the Spiritual Life Game—is to Refresh (I use a capital "R" to emphasize the importance of this practice) as often as 10 to 100 times each day. When you refresh a room, you clear out the old and bring in the new. When you refresh plants and flowers, you snip off dead leaves and give new water and food to promote better growth and renewed energy.

To Refresh during The Game, you'll follow a very simple process. First, stop whatever you're doing and cut out distractions. Then, close your eyes, inhale a few times, and allow your entire body to relax.

Look at this time while you're Refreshing—inhaling and exhaling—as idling the engine of your mind. This is the time when you allow old energy and thoughts to drain away, and let new ones filter into your mind.

Refresh when you end one activity and before you start another. Refresh when you feel thoughts and emotions clamoring for your attention, taking you away from yourself. Refresh when you want to be reminded of your higher purpose and the meaning of your life. Refresh when it all gets to be too much. Refresh when you want to relieve stress, overwork, and the chaotic pressures of day-to-day existence. And remember to give yourself points in The Spiritual Life Game for every time you remember to Refresh.

Game-player Maris Lamberg describes when he Refreshed on an especially stressful day.

He says:

> *On a day that my stress level went through the roof, and anger, frustration, fear, and worries flooded my mind, I just stopped what I was doing and spent several minutes taking deep breaths and letting my mind slow down. I shifted my focus to the present moment instead of all the disasters that seemed to loom ahead. With this slowing-down, I found real peace of mind and clarity of thought. Everything became manageable again. Entering this brief space defused all my anxieties and returned me to myself.*

A special rule for The Spiritual Life Game is:
Refresh regularly, frequently, and at the
beginning and end of each new task or activity.

Putting the Vehicle into Service

If you think of yourself and your body, mind, emotions, and spirit as a composite vehicle for aligning with your purpose, you'll understand why it's essential to add giving service to all life to your Spiritual Life Game. Giving service tests how earnest you are about playing The Game and winning your life. Serving all life instead of merely looking out for Number One opens up a world of possibilities.

There's a quote I like to read to the clients in my coaching classes who are about to play The Game for the first time. It's from a book of interviews between a questioner (Q) and a spiritual teacher (A). The book's title is *I Am That,* by Sri Nisargadatta Maharaj (Acorn Press, 1977). I'd like to offer this spiritual wisdom for your reflection. I think it speaks beautifully to the expansiveness of serving all life.

> A: What happened to your energy? Where did it go? Did you not scatter it over so many contradictory desires and pursuits? You don't have an infinite supply of energy.
>
> Q: Why not?
>
> A: Your aims are small and low. They do not call for more. Only God's energy is infinite—because He wants nothing for Himself. Be like Him and all your desires will be fulfilled. The higher your aims and vaster your desires, the more energy you will have for their fulfillment. Desire the good of all and the universe will work with you. But if you want your own pleasure, you must earn it the hard way. Before desiring, deserve.

I particularly draw my clients' attention to the last part of this passage. As a regular practice, we begin each coaching session by saying the affirmation: *"We dedicate what we're about to do to the service of all life."* This gives everything a sense of spiritual purpose. When people are only interested in serving themselves, they're contracted, and in many cases, lead very small lives. Regardless of their apparent accomplishments, inside they're diminished.

As you repeatedly affirm your dedication to service, watch your life and the universe align to support you in ways you never imagined possible. Your aims will transform from small and low to vast and high.

A special rule for The Spiritual Life Game
is to repeat the following affirmation:
I dedicate what I'm about to do to the service of all life.

Spiritual Life Game Exercises

Use the activities described with the special rules above if you decide to make The Spiritual Life Game one of the three to five aspects of life you want to improve in 90 days. Also, design The Spiritual Life Game by using The Game's basic elements described in Part III of this book: goals, To-Be and Not-To-Be lists, points, prizes, rules, Before-and-After Displays, essays, skills, rewards, consequences, deadlines, partners, and coaches.

If you're adopting a special practice or system for The Spiritual Life Game, give yourself points for using it. An example of a consequence for not achieving goals in The Spiritual Life Game would be that if you haven't kept your spiritual commitments during the month, you could go to a church or whatever organization you said you'd attend regularly and address everyone you meet there as "Oh, Superior One."

Refer to **TheGameInteractive.com** Website for more ideas and coaching specifically targeted to improving your performance in The Spiritual Life Game.

Use the information in Part I of this book in the chapters "Time," "Structure," "Affinity," "Community," and "Purpose" to balance and coordinate The Spiritual Life Game with your overall Game plan.

✳ ✳ ✳

In the next chapter, you're going to switch gears from spiritual awareness to mental alertness, and delve into the mysteries of your mind.

✳ ✳ ✳

✦ CHAPTER 11 ✦

Your Mind

It's usually not too pleasant when people play mind games and try to trick and manipulate themselves or others. This chapter will teach you how to play The Mind Game. Unlike typical mind games, it will free you to fulfill your purpose in life and help you become all you've ever wanted to be.

Look at the list of mental games you may be playing with yourself now to see if any of them describe you:

- You're often inattentive, distracted, unfocused, and easily bored.

- You obsess and agitate over problems and situations that aren't under your control.

- You give up easily and don't finish much of anything.

- You've been accused of being self-absorbed.

- You often criticize yourself and put yourself down.

- You've been daydreaming your life away instead of taking action.

If any of these habits describe you, consider replacing the mental games you've been playing with The Mind Game for 90 days. In addition to the special rules and principles I'll be discussing in this chapter, you can use any programs, books, systems, philosophies, or therapies that align with your higher purpose. Just plug them into The Mind Game's technology of To-Be or Not-To-Be lists, points, and scoring systems. The new skills, habits, and attitudes you'll acquire by playing The Mind Game will positively impact everything else you do in The Game and in your life.

Controlling Your Mind

One of the fundamental challenges of the mind is its inability to focus. The Game's technology, which has you focus on your purpose instead of being galvanized by negative emotions, is a powerful tool for taking control of your mind. If you're like most of us, you're kidding yourself if you think you currently have your mind under control. If you did, you'd be producing astonishing results in ways that bring great satisfaction and contentment without exerting a lot of internal effort.

When your self-talk switches from obsessing over your problems to finding creative ways for furthering your purpose, you'll be taking the driver's seat in your own life. To get there, you have to focus like a laser beam on the goals you've set for your Game. In "The Gold Medal," by James Bauman, Ph.D. (*Psychology Today,* May/June 2000), this sports psychologist for the U.S. Olympic Training Center calls the mind the software controlling the hardware of our flesh, bone, and muscles. He says that the Olympians' mental muscles are what set them apart from other athletes. Dr. Bauman cites a 1986 study done by Albert Bandura, Ph.D., at Stanford University that found that while most of us worry about things we can't control, successful athletes focus only on the cues or stimuli within their control.

Increasing Your Attention Span

As you play The Mind Game, you'll be conducting some experiments and will undoubtedly be surprised to see how easily distracted you are. Your level of inattentiveness explains why you have such a hard time getting anything meaningful accomplished. Playing The Game and picking up velocity increases your attention span. Getting out of your head and into action is the powerful tool you'll use to counteract boredom, distraction, and mental agitation.

Daydreaming Your Life Away

The addiction to daydreaming, to fantasizing about the past and the future, is one of the fundamental habits that has stopped you from being effective. As shown earlier, if you examine your day, you'll notice that you spend very little time in the present. This means that instead of taking action, you're thinking, cogitating, agitating, and doing the proverbial contemplation of your navel.

Daydreaming is easily distinguished from creative visualization or artistic creation, where the mind is using imagination and intuition to access the heart and spirit. Creative imagination stimulates action and places the artist so squarely in the present that he or she even loses track of time and becomes totally absorbed in the work. This is definitely not the same as daydreaming, which is escapist in nature.

Daydreaming is your mind's inane, endless, repetitive chatter—the stories you've been repeating to yourself since childhood. Daydreaming saps and blocks your energy. The good news is that when you manage to break your addiction to daydreaming, you can devote all the time and energy you've been devoting to this habit to fulfilling your higher purpose and accomplishing your goals.

Game-player Steve Powilatis says, "For most of my life, I've been thinking instead of doing. I've been paralyzed, unable to truly take action and move forward in an accomplished manner. In the 90 days I played The Game, I've shifted from living inside my head to *doing*."

If you'd like to experience Steve's results, practice a special rule for playing The Mind Game: ***Stop daydreaming.***

Doing What Your Mind Presents

Your mind is a powerful instrument. When it's convinced that you're serious about winning your life and are motivated by love, it will do much more than merely cooperate. As you play The Game, your mind will amaze you with how efficient, productive, and in tune with life it can help you become.

When your mind presents an idea, try acting on it as immediately as you can. This isn't the same as impulsively acting on every thought. Instead, you're short-circuiting the daydreaming habit by taking action. As you refine this habit of doing what your mind offers you, you're training it to stop presenting rambling thoughts. It's as if your mind starts saying, "Oh, you're really going to act on these thoughts. I'd better make sure they're good ones."

When I practice doing whatever my mind presents, I find that I'm decreasing the agitation that delaying and doubting myself causes. I've learned that waiting costs me vitality, peace, love, and happiness. Doing something as soon as I think of it takes me through a doorway to the present where all things work together. I develop a profound connection of mind, body, and spirit when I trust my mind to be expanded by the love I'm putting into fulfilling my potential. I've learned that I can rely on my mind to prompt me toward achieving my goals.

I discovered the power of immediately acting upon what my mind presents when I wanted to get into better physical shape.

I couldn't get to the gym quickly every time I thought about it, so I decided to experiment with immediately acting upon my mind's intuitive sense of what's best for me. Whenever I thought of exercising, instead of letting myself daydream and lament over not going to the gym, I promptly did something active such as push-ups or sit-ups. I was surprised to notice that after a while, thoughts of exercise didn't agitate me. I also stopped thinking about the gym unless I was actually *in* the gym. I had become present to what my body needed in each moment. Acting upon my thoughts had helped me do this.

At this point, I was developing unity and love between my mind and body. My mind was guiding me to what was important for me, and I was following through by doing it.

You can acquire this kind of teamwork between your mind, heart, and body in 90 days. The beauty of playing The Game is that you'll begin to use your mind as a resource instead of fighting against it. You'll stop regarding your mind as a source of distraction and recognize that it's presenting you with your true priorities. As you focus your life toward doing the things you love, your mind will help you develop a passion for these positive habits and behaviors by making you think of them frequently.

Game-player Ritchie Gomez offers advice he learned by playing The Game. He says, "The moment you have a thought is when you also have the energy and momentum to accomplish it."

A special rule for The Mind Game is:
As immediately as possible, convert thoughts into action by doing what your mind presents.

Your Mind Will Love You for This

Here's the really fun part. Your mind loves to be purposeful. Like a state-of-the-art computer, it thrives on strutting out its fancy capabilities and amazing you by doing the impossible. When its energy is harnessed and aimed in a positive direction, your mind is no longer plagued with boredom, meandering thoughts, inattentiveness, and unfocused energy. You and your mind are going to develop a solid partnership and have a great time playing The Mind Game.

Your mind is like an unruly child who feels more secure when the parent sets up structures, rules, and discipline. When your mind is clear that it has no choice but to do as it's instructed, that you're serious and not dithering around, it becomes a very happy camper. Your mind loves it when you're no longer changing your focus every few seconds, and it hunkers down to get serious about fulfilling your desires. If your mind can't trust you to know what you want, why should it use all its powers of creativity to support you? Why not just continue to snooze, fantasize, or be lazy and inattentive?

One of the great benefits of developing a positive relationship with your mind is that as you play The Game, your mind may start to wake you up earlier in the morning. It's as if your mind is now convinced that there's an important reason for you to get out of bed. If you're spending your day wastefully, your mind won't wake up for much of that and will allow you to sleep more than you need, or to daydream.

What Are You Telling Yourself?

The other destructive habit you've developed in addition to daydreaming is the tendency to let your mental chatter destroy your self-esteem and morale. This is what is known as negative self-talk. In 1987, Albert Ellis, Ph.D., the founder of rational emotive therapy, showed in his studies that negative self-talk increases distraction and decreases performance in athletes.

What you're telling yourself is seriously affecting how well you fulfill your potential as a human being.

Ingrained in you from childhood are certain beliefs that you hold about yourself, such as that you're bad, lazy, a screw-up, too fat, too thin, uncoordinated, or any number of negative things. When your mind repeats these thoughts, you're constantly looking for and automatically accepting as proof anything that shows that these unpleasant views are true.

Even though it's clear to everyone around you, based on how you present yourself to the world today, that you're anything but ugly, selfish, stupid, or a failure, your mind considers your accomplishments to be exceptions. Your mind convinces you that anyone who sees you in a brighter light than you view yourself must be either foolish or blinded by love. You busily deny all proof that as an adult you don't exhibit the negative traits you internalized about yourself as a child. Instead, your mind convinces you that the truth could come out any day now. So you lay low, live half-heartedly, and hide your light. By doing so, no one can uncover what an imposter you are.

If you're not careful and attentive to this pattern, you'll use The Game and your To-Be and Not-To-Be lists to prove that there's something wrong with you. That's why one of the general rules of The Game is that for 90 days you don't criticize yourself. It's high time to focus your mind on what's great and terrific about you.

To counteract negative self-talk, go back to the statement of purpose you made earlier, and apply the goals you designed for your personalized Game to write affirmations. These can be statements such as: *I am a highly focused and attentive person,* or *I create harmony, love, and goodwill in every aspect of my life and with everyone I meet.* Write these positive affirmations and post them in places where they'll remind you to repeat them. Say these affirmations throughout the day, and replace negative mental chatter with words that inspire images of the great human being that you truly are.

Ken Doyle, one of the master coaches in **TheCoaching-Program.com,** says that using affirmations has helped him immensely in focusing attention on his higher purpose rather than allowing his mind to wander into negative self-talk. He creates and repeats affirmations all day long and has them running through his mind like a steady stream as he works, exercises, and goes about his daily life. He finds that they strengthen his resolve and keep him operating from a place of love and service rather than being preoccupied with nitpicking or pettiness.

A special rule for The Mind Game is:
Write your higher purpose and goals
as affirmations, and repeat them frequently.

Who's the Star of Your Daydreaming Show?

You know the movie that's incessantly playing in your head? The one where you're the hero and everybody else is a villain? The one where you get the girl or guy who sees your true worth, falls in love with you, and becomes your love slave forever? The one where your boss finally notices how hard you work and gives you a big raise and an office with windows? Who's the star of these shows?

Me. Me. Me. Me. And only me.

Daydreaming fosters an incredible amount of self-absorption. There's a good portion of your day where you walk around wondering what other people are thinking about you.

Guess what? You're flattering yourself. These people aren't thinking about you at all. They're thinking about themselves. Their minds and stories are rotating around their own lives and concerns.

One way to pull out of this tendency toward self-absorption is to empower your mind by giving it a significantly larger problem other than whether or not you can include cigars on your expense account or whether your fellow employees are hogging the refrigerator in the company kitchen. Giving your mind a problem that is beyond you refines your thinking by taking you out of the sleepy comfort zone of mediocrity.

When your mind has a fully engaging and energizing problem that aligns with your higher purpose, it disappears in order to work on it. Then your mind forgets about its habits of daydreaming and self-criticism. It's now preoccupied with the new and bigger challenge.

If you don't allow your mind to operate at full capacity, boredom and serious problems set in. So your mind creates negative challenges to give you something to do and keep you alive. The old saying is true: *An idle mind is the devil's workshop.* Your mind becomes self-destructive when you haven't given it big enough challenges.

There's not much of value in the world for a mind that thinks it knows everything. When you give the mind large problems, you'll move into the mode where you can start expecting the unexpected and leave room for miracles to occur.

A fundamental human desire is to gain contentment. This isn't the same as boredom, where there's nothing meaningful to do or think about. Instead, contentment arises when your mind is fully engaged in something as big as giving service to all life.

Mother Teresa had a really big problem. Dr. Martin Luther King, Jr., had a really big problem. Mohandas Gandhi had a really big problem. Jesus took on a really big problem. By contrast, you and I are petty. How big are our problems, really? How low and small are our aims?

When you give yourself a big enough problem, you'll discover that you have all the time in the world to work on resolving it. While daydreaming your life away, you've been spending time creating excuses for why your life hasn't worked out in the way you thought it should. A mind that's addressing a very high level of problem will create a bigger life to deal with it.

A special rule of The Mind Game is:
Create bigger problems for your mind to solve.

Start with Bigger Challenges in Your Daily Life

Take a look at how you currently do your job. How busy are you really? If you mind isn't fully engaged with your work, then step up to the plate and take on a larger role inside of the work you're doing. This isn't the same thing as asking for a promotion. It's you choosing to be responsible for making your day fuller, more enjoyable, and more productive, instead of retreating into your own mind and repeating your old, unoriginal fantasies. Think of what a difference it would make if your boss noticed that you were spending your mental energy scheming up better ways to do your job.

If you're someone who's using your computer to play games or send out countless e-mail jokes and messages, there's nothing inherently wrong with these activities, but it's the equivalent of sucking on an electronic pacifier. You're robbing your community and yourself of the satisfaction that comes from doing something much more challenging, rewarding, and engaging.

As you shift your focus to a bigger problem, you'll be amazed to see how you've been rewarding yourself for devoting enormous amounts of time and attention to complaining. Remember, a general rule in The Game is that there's no complaining for 90 days. You can give yourself a point every time you think about complaining and don't. While playing The Mind Game, you'll be making a paradigm shift in which your mind stops looking for what's missing and brings to your attention the gifts and talents that have lain dormant and unused. Not using these gifts has made you a loser in the game of life. Now you're going to become a winner.

Create Space for Your Mind to Just "Be"

In The Mind Game, you'll be doing many meaningful activities as you focus on your mental processes and determine how they've hurt or could become helpful to you. You'll also be moving with velocity as you kick into high gear to improve three to five areas of your life in 90 days. This makes it imperative that you create space for your mind to rest and regroup—to just be.

In the last chapter, I introduced the process I call Refresh. It's imperative for playing The Mind Game successfully. This practice will allow you to watch how your mind operates and to see thought happening. It will take you into deeper and quieter levels as you become more and more present to each moment of life. As you increase the number of times you Refresh, you'll begin to see how your mind and life are working together. During this 90 days, you can notice that you're having questions answered that you've always wondered about.

Game-player James Kirchner says:

> *While playing The Game, I found that I was terrified of success. I made a great start only to find that I soon began tripping myself up. I allowed anyone and everyone to get into my head and tell me how silly it was to play The Game. I listened to negative voices and didn't allow myself to do well.*
>
> *The one or two things I did do enabled me to pull out of this downward spiral. I used the process Sarano taught us of stopping to Refresh, and I meditated. This is how I discovered that at the root of my problems was the fact that I feared success. It didn't matter what the success was— whether it involved learning how to become a great dancer, a good worker, or have satisfying relationships—I was afraid of it.*
>
> *I'm continuing to work on this issue within myself. But now I have the tools and practices I need with The Game to help me overcome this lifelong problem.*

When you Refresh, it allows you to slip between the cracks of your life, discover what's really true about you, and go into meaningful action to do something about the blockages your mind has used to keep yourself limited.

A special rule for The Mind Game is:
Refresh frequently.

THE MIND GAME EXERCISES

In addition to using the activities described with the special rules above, do the following exercise if you decide to make The Mind Game one of the three to five aspects of life you want to improve in 90 days. Also, design The Mind Game by using The Game's basic elements described in Part III of this book: goals, To-Be and Not-To-Be lists, points, prizes, rules, Before-and-After Displays, essays, skills, rewards, consequences, deadlines, partners, and coaches.

If you're adopting a special philosophy or system for The Mind Game, give yourself points for using it. An example of a consequence for not achieving goals in The Mind Game would be that every time you find yourself putting things off that your mind has presented, you have to say out loud within earshot of other people, in your whiniest voice, "I don't wanna …" Refer to **TheGameInteractive.com** Website for more ideas and coaching specifically targeted to improving your performance in The Mind Game.

Use the information in Part I of this book in the chapters "Time," "Structure," "Affinity," "Community," and "Purpose" to balance and coordinate The Mind Game with your overall Game plan.

EXERCISE: HOW LONG IS MY ATTENTION SPAN?

To do this exercise, use a watch or clock with a second-hand, and look at it while you allow your mind to focus on nothing but the moving hand. When a thought enters your mind, notice how many seconds have elapsed as a measure of your attention span. If you're watching the clock the entire time and thinking that you're not thinking anything, then give yourself a score of zero. It's not unusual for people to have attention spans of less than seven seconds when they first try this exercise. Continue to practice it during your Mind Game, and watch how your attention span increases and your ability to focus grows.

✳ ✳ ✳

Now we'll be focusing on how you can greatly increase the scope and breadth of your resources through the use of tools and technology.

✳ ✳ ✳

★ CHAPTER 12 ★

Your Tools

The world of technology is simultaneously exciting, intriguing, complex, and intimidating. Yet many of us harbor a secret shame that we haven't really programmed our VCRs correctly. We feel mentally deficient about never being sure which settings to use on our microwave ovens. Lines form behind us at automatic bank teller machines as we struggle to remember which buttons to push. We marvel at the many bells and whistles on shiny, new technogadgets we've rushed out to buy because we heard they'd save us a lot of time.

If you want to know more about the technology and equipment you currently have, or would like these mysterious creations to fulfill on their many promises, then you'll definitely want to win your life with this chapter. For 90 days, you can explore, probe, study, take apart, put back together, have repaired, and experiment with the marvels of the 21st century. So, pull out those buried treasures you've hidden in your closets because you never could figure out how to operate them. Find those owner's manuals, still in their plastic wrappers, which you've shoved into drawers. Open up those hoods and look under them. Welcome to The Tool Game.

In my coaching classes, I ask clients: How good of a tool-using animal are you? This always gets a good laugh, because when we compare ourselves to the efficiency of chimpanzees, who make tools out of sticks and rocks and manage to feed themselves and their families, we seem to be a little lower on the evolutionary rung than we'd like to be. Tools were created by humans to extend our reach, increase our efficiency, and expand our abilities. To do all those things, we have to master their use. But something has gone awry. We're out of balance. Science has invented and perfected tools faster than we can learn how to operate them. For 90 days, you're going to have the opportunity to play catch-up with technology.

The Tool Game restores your equilibrium and helps you climb up on that technology horse and learn how to ride it. Instead of running out to buy more tools and increasing your frustration with them, you'll discover how to use them to their fullest capacity. Rather than having technology cause you more stress, you'll feel calm in the face of buttons, clickers, and other forms of wizardry. You'll learn the limitations as well as the possibilities of the tools in your repertoire, and see how to use them proficiently to increase your productivity and make your life easier.

Sound good? Well, read on to get some basic principles that will guide you through the maze of tools and technology available to you right now.

Finding Your Tools

To play The Tool Game, the first thing you'll do is inventory exactly what tools you currently have access to at home, work, school, or your local library. These would be items such as personal computers, televisions, VCRs, clock radios, tape recorders, CD players, automobile cruise controls, microwave ovens, automatic coffee makers, small appliances, timers—anything electrical, digital, or computerized that's supposed to be making your life better or easier in some way. Go ahead—work your way from home to car to work to local library (where you have access to many tools for free), and list them all.

Then look at your list and refer back to the statement of higher purpose you created in Part I of this book. Out of all the tools you currently have access to, which ones seem to be essential for fulfilling your higher purpose and accomplishing your goals? If you have some ideas about the aspects of life you'll be focusing on in The Game, which tools will be necessary for managing your time more effectively and improving those areas? Narrow down your list of available tools to ten that fit the criteria of helping you make your life more meaningful and satisfying in 90 days.

> **A special rule for The Tool Game is:**
> *Select ten tools that will help you*
> *fulfill your higher purpose.*

How Proficient Are You with Your Tools?

Next, using a scale of one to ten, rate yourself on how proficient you are with each of these tools that will improve the quality and purpose of your life.

A rating of ten is the highest. A ten means you're a master, a whiz. You should be giving lessons or teaching courses about this tool; you could have written the manual yourself. A rating of one is the lowest. You're absolutely dismal with this tool. It's hidden like a monster under your bed; this tool scares the living daylights out of you.

You'll probably be somewhere at the lower end of the rating scale for a few tools, and in the middle for most. If you're like me, you've managed to somewhat figure out what your tools can do and what you can do with them, but you suspect that there's at least 50 percent more available for you to learn. You discovered this secret when you accidentally hit the wrong button, or you watched in awe as some 12-year-old child tapped at a computer. In this moment of revelation, you saw menus and programs pop up that could have been transmissions from Mars for all you knew.

Studying Your Tools

Now that you've decided which ten tools you'll focus on learning how to use and have rated your efficiency with them, you'll need to find the manuals for these ten tools. Here are some places you might try first:

- In the bottom of boxes that the appliances or equipment came in, probably underneath the Styrofoam, or buried under those little clinging things that look like maggots and spill out all over the floor.

- In the kitchen, desk, or file cabinet drawer where you throw everything you think you might need someday.

- In the garage, basement, or attic, behind the last place you'd ever think to look.

In spite of your best efforts, if you can't find the owner's manuals for these ten technological wonders, then you'll need to call or write to the manufacturer or store where you bought them and admit your negligence. Tell them they must mail the manuals to you quickly because in 90 days, you're going to be so proficient that you'll teach classes on how to use this equipment and direct hundreds of new customers their way. The manuals could be in your mailbox the next day!

After you've located the operating instructions for your ten important toys, start a file folder labeled "Never Lose This

Again," place them in it, and study the manuals one at a time. This is where you have to be brave and remember that short of being electrocuted if you stick your finger in the sockets, these tools can't hurt you.

Probe, explore, and experiment with your tools, following their carefully written instructions. If this doesn't work, and you still can't figure out how to operate them, call those toll-free numbers listed in the manual, or better yet, invite people to lunch who can teach you how to use these pieces of equipment. That way, you'll have meals, companionship . . . and you'll learn how to use your tools.

A special rule for The Tool Game is:
Study the manuals, and learn
how to proficiently use your tools.

The Skills Your Tools Require

You'll need to do more than master your ten tools. You'll have to improve your skills for using them more efficiently. How good is it to understand your computer's word processing program if you can only type five words a minute with two fingers?

Your next phase of tool mastery is to analyze the skills you'll need to become proficient with your tools. This might mean getting faster at punching keys on your calculator. Or practicing your typing to become faster and more agile. Or learning the shortcuts on your keyboard to cut down on the number of strokes you use for word-processing functions. Or actually inputting all the phone numbers you frequently dial into your cell phone's memory. For example, Gino Coppola, one of our master coaching program instructors, has acquired an exquisite mastery of his Palm Pilot. In addition to using this tool as an effective way for planning and managing his time, Gino can contact anyone he needs at any time with the information he's programmed into this tool. Think of how much more efficient you'll be when you've complemented your tools with increased effectiveness.

After you've figured out what skills are necessary to operate your tools better, rate yourself on how proficient you are with these skills. In 90 days, you can rate yourself again and show the progress on your Before-and-After displays and the essay you send to me about your magnificent accomplishments.

Now You're Really Going for It

You've managed to master ten of your currently available tools. Now you're going to select three entirely new tools that you believe will help you fulfill your higher purpose and achieve the goals of your Game. You'll either buy or borrow these tools, and master their use in 90 days. This is where you stretch. It's your opportunity to actually have tools arrive with operating instructions intact and accessible. It's your moment to shine. It's time for you to conquer your fears of new technology and show yourself and the world that nothing, not even a DVD player, can stop you from reaching for the stars.

One of our Game-players, Dave Rogers, wrote this in his essay after playing The Tool Game for 90 days:

> I've discovered all kinds of cool stuff on The Internet, as well as for the Palm systems. Each morning, I go to a site that reformats many magazines and newspapers for the Palm Pilot. Most important, I get to read a men's magazine for the joke of the day, as well as articles on "how to drive her wild." So when I have a few minutes of waiting or delay, I can use it to catch up on all the news.

As one of the three new tools you choose to master for The Tool Game, I strongly suggest that you make one of them the use of the Worldwide Web and the Internet. Even if you're already logged on, consider devoting some additional time and attention to exploring the phenomenal level of planetary communication offered on the Internet. In these times, the Internet offers the opportunity for establishing communities all over the globe to support and further your higher purpose.

Remember that you'll need to go on the Internet and submit the essay about your accomplishments at our Website—**TheGameInteractive.com**—after your 90-day Game. This will make you eligible for the grand cash prizes, coaching opportunities, and special offers.

A special rule for The Tool Game is:
Select three new tools to master that will bring more meaning to your life. Make one of them the Internet.

Where Did I Put That Tool?

As you inventory your tools, also be looking for ways to organize them for more efficient and frequent use. Are there some tools you have in one part of your home that would get more use in another part? If you spend a lot of time in the kitchen, would you log on to the Internet between chores if your laptop computer was easily accessible there rather than in an office where you rarely have time to go?

Where's the best place to store your tools when they're not in use? Where could you file those operating instructions and the numbers you should call for service and repair? Do you have a spot for the boxes that equipment and appliances came in so you can return them to the factory if you need to?

A special rule for The Tool Game is:
Organize your tools.

Tool Gratitude

During the 90 days of The Tool Game, make it a point to treat your tools with greater respect. Have them repaired. Get them updated and expanded. Store them properly. Express gratitude for the many gifts tools bring into your life.

When a team of friends from our coaching classes decided to go to Africa in the summer of 2000 to climb Mt. Kilimanjaro, they learned firsthand the value of tools and technology. Our coaching program master instructor, Dr. Martin Kettelhut, who went on this adventure, says, "One lesson I learned on this trip was the importance of being properly equipped. Having the best techniques and tools available and using them masterfully makes all the difference in quality, safety, smoothness, and the vividness of life's experiences."

Mike Haynes also climbed the great mountain and had this to share about his gratitude for tools.

He says:

> Having the right technology at the right time turned what could potentially have been very uncomfortable and dangerous situations into times when I felt good about myself and enjoyed the moments.
>
> On our second day in Africa, the right technology was a simple iodine pill we had to dissolve in water for 20 minutes before we could drink it. Without this pill, we'd become violently ill and wouldn't have been able to continue our hike up the mountain.
>
> On day five of our African adventure, we left at midnight for the final ascent to the top of Mt. Kilimanjaro. When that hike started, the technology we needed was a lamp attached to a headband so we could see the rocky pathway.
>
> Traveling in Africa made me realize that everything I've learned in coaching classes about the importance of mastering technology was true. I also became more grateful for

some tools I'd previously taken for granted. In the Masai village we visited, the children were both amazed and amused by watching themselves on the screen of a video camera we'd brought with us. They gawked at a ballpoint pen cylinder moving in and out of its tube. This trip made me grateful for lights, clothes, heat, running water, and toothpaste. My eyes were opened and my life enlightened to the way tools allowed me to be present for my African experience and enjoy my climb up the mountain.

A special rule for The Tool Game is:
*Show gratitude for your tools by
taking better care of them.*

It Starts with You

If you've read this far and are still thinking things such as: *I'm just not a computer person; I'm too old; this is for the younger generation; technology is the wave for the future; I'm from the old school . . .* then you're passing up more opportunities then you could have ever imagined. For one thing, you're probably being passed over for many things that you might have desired or appreciated. For example:

- Others are promoted at work because they're more technologically proficient than you are.

- Classmates win scholarships you wanted because they have greater access to research and knowledge over the Internet than you do.

- You're losing income because competitors use the most state-of-the-art customer service tools and you don't.

- Other writers are getting published, because agents and editors can contact them by e-mail, receive and edit their manuscripts on disk, and promote them with live chats on the Internet.

- Your artist and entrepreneur friends have been able to quit their day jobs because they're selling their products at Internet auctions and on their Websites, while you're struggling to pay for your supplies and travel expenses so you can rent booths at art fairs and flea markets.

As you decide whether to play The Tool Game, take a long, hard look at what mastery of your tools could do for you in the short term and throughout the rest of your life.

Tool Game Exercises

Do the activities included with the special rules above if you decide to make The Tool Game one of the three to five aspects of life you want to improve in 90 days. Also, design The Tool Game by using The Game's basic elements described in Part III of this book: goals, To-Be and Not-To-Be lists, points, prizes, rules, Before-and-After Displays, essays, skills, rewards, consequences, deadlines, partners, and coaches.

If you're adopting a special training or system for The Tool Game, give yourself points for using it. An example of a consequence for not achieving goals in The Tool Game would be that if you don't master a certain tool you committed to learn for The Tool Game, you'll donate it to charity or give it to someone who will put it better use. Refer to **TheGame-Interactive.com** Website for more ideas and coaching specifically targeted to improving your performance in The Tool Game.

Use the information in Part I of this book in the chapters "Time," "Structure," "Affinity," "Community," and "Purpose" to balance and coordinate The Tool Game with your overall Game plan.

✳ ✳ ✳

Now that you're committed to becoming a technical wizard, you'll want to turn your attention to your inner and outer environment to see what you'd like to improve in the world around you.

✳ ✳ ✳

★ Chapter 13 ★

Your Environment

Look around you. How cluttered, disorganized, and messy are the areas where you live, work, go to school, or play? Can you find everything you want or need easily? Are things that are no longer useful to you still taking up space? If what you're seeing right now isn't pretty, then you'll be happy to join your fellow pack rats and disorganized cohorts in playing The Environment Game.

But what if the paragraph above doesn't describe you? Organization, cleanliness, and orderliness are your middle names. *A place for everything and everything in its place* is your motto. If only *they* would take care of the office/room/neighborhood/planet, then the world would be much better.

Guess what? The Environment Game is for *you*, too. You're about to look in the mirror and realize that the elusive, nameless, faceless *they* are staring back at you. This is where you get to become a master Game-player and operate as if your life is critical to the planet. Because no matter how small and insignificant you might consider yourself to be, you *do* make a difference, and you're going to prove this to yourself in only 90 days.

Your Current Environment Games

See if these statements describe the games you're playing with your environment:

- Let's see how disorganized and dirty my space can get before I absolutely have to clean it up.

- Visitors are coming, so I'd better clean my house and not let anybody know what a slob I really am.

- When I move to my new home, I absolutely refuse to carry all this junk with me, so it's going to be much cleaner.

- If I dump this trash out here, nobody will ever know.

- The next time people ask for money to save the rainforests or clean up the city parks, I'm going to make a donation, and then I've done my fair share.

Are your environment games giving you a sense of accomplishment and peacefulness? As you survey your space, are you seeing an accurate reflection of you as a person? Someone who desires and deserves respect?

The Structure of Your Environment

Did you realize that you may have structured your environments to reinforce whatever you feel most insecure about or fear the most? If, deep down, you think of yourself as a lazy, ugly, selfish, or disorganized person, even though you project a completely different image to the world, your environments may be set up to make you believe the lies you've been telling about yourself since childhood.

By doing so, when you sit at your desk, if it's buried in your psyche that you're a failure, you'll place evidence of your mistakes where you can look at them every day. When you play The Environment Game, you're going to observe what you've put in your line of vision every day. Then you'll rearrange, replace, and discard whatever isn't calling you to be your best. You'll get rid of things that aren't projecting the excellent human being you really are.

For example, a simple principle that's taught in the ancient Chinese practice of Feng Shui is that you shouldn't leave dirty laundry in view of your bed because it busies your mind with what you have to do instead of allowing you to rest.

Also, you may not be aware of the tremendous sensual impact your environment is having on you constantly. What you see, hear, touch, smell, and taste is bombarding your mind with images that are affecting you.

One day I was working at my table and found myself drifting off into a fantasy about a woman. Well, this isn't too unusual a daydream for a man to have, but it surprised me, because I hadn't been thinking about this woman or my sexual needs at all. I'd been absorbed and focused on my work. As I began to trace my thoughts to see what could have triggered them, I noticed that to my side, on the edge of the table, I'd left a magazine. On the back cover was an advertisement with a risqué photo of a woman on it. I was surprised to realize that having this little bit of clutter in my environment had subtly and subliminally shifted my attention away from the task at hand. I had not set up my environment to support what I was committed to accomplishing.

In the Environment Game, it's essential that you objectively take a look at where you live. Examine these areas for clutter:

- Your house and each room or closet

- Where you work: your office, desk, workshop, and break rooms

- Your social surroundings: where you go for entertainment, education, or exercise

Ask yourself if these spaces are currently set up as an extension of your self-image and your life. What do you have in your bedroom that causes the end of each day to be more peaceful and relaxing? What items are on your desk that stimulate your thinking in the most creative and positive ways? What photos and artwork are on your walls? Do you display pictures of people who inspire you and remind you of your higher purpose? What colors have you painted your house to put yourself and visitors into an open and loving state of mind?

What about the current state of your car? When you get into it, does it uplift your spirits or make you feel like a slob? Does this environment make you and others feel comfortable, respected, and honored?

Environment is a structure that summons thoughts, feelings, emotions, and behaviors. If you've allowed your environments to be places that have just "happened," or you've arbitrarily slapped them together, they'll lack cohesion and even work against all you say you want to be.

A special rule for The Environment Game is:
Analyze all the spaces you currently occupy to
see which ones don't support who you want to be.

Rethinking Your Environments

If you take 90 days to rethink, plan, and reorganize your environments, then they will reflect and further your higher purpose and bring you and others greater satisfaction and peace.

You *are* your environments. They're merely reflections of your own state of consciousness and view of yourself and the world. The bad news is that you've created your messy and unproductive spaces. The good news is that now you can re-create them to offer you more joy and efficiency. Shifting and reshaping your environments will free you in ways you never imagined.

One of **TheCoachingProgram.com's** clients went home after attending one of our weekend seminars and tackled an issue that had caused consternation for seven years between his wife and himself. All this time, he'd disliked his house and had ignored all the things that made him uncomfortable. Avoidance took much more energy than doing something about the things he wanted changed. To play The Environment Game, my client ripped out his entire kitchen and living room and enlisted his family and friends to help him completely redecorate, redesign, and create a whole new space for his family and himself. He produced a phenomenal transformation within a very short time. At the end of his Game, this man was proud to show us the Before-and-After display photos of his home.

Other Game-players have cleaned out those drawers, closets, garages, and attics of items that were taking up space and possibly could be of greater use to others. Game-player Michael Haynes says that his garage had been messy and dirty 365 days of the year. Every morning, he'd open the door from his house to his garage and think, *I sure wish this place was cleaner/neater/more organized.* When Mike played The Environment Game, he thoroughly cleaned and reorganized his garage. Now he walks through the door each day and says, "All right! This place looks great!" He's found that transforming the things he'd always found to be sources of irritation into reminders of his accomplishments is a lot better way to start his days and live his life.

After you've rid yourself of the clutter, you can re-analyze spaces to decide thoughtfully and carefully what should go in them that will truly reflect the fine human being you are.

Game-player Loy Gotham painted a garden with wisterias, butterflies, and bees on her bedroom wall. This peaceful and beautiful setting was much more aligned with who she is than blank walls or pictures that didn't convey her originality and creativity.

Hidden Clutter

Don't think that because you can't *see* your clutter, it's not having an effect on you. In closets, garages, and attics, you'll find things you thought had been lost forever. How effective can you be when you don't know where you put things that you say are important to you? By cleaning out hidden messes and chaotic spaces, you'll be in harmony with your environment instead of having it work against you.

If you're someone who can't bear to part with your possessions, ask your communities of family members and friends to help you discard "stuff." If it's absolutely unbearable for you to get rid of your beloved high school football jersey or those frayed blouses that no longer fit, get yourself out of the house and ask others to surgically remove the bricks from your memory lanes.

A special rule for The Environment Game is:
Clean up the visible AND hidden
messes in your environments.

Changing the Habits That Affect Your Environment

It's not going to do much good for you to play The Environment Game if you don't change the habits and behaviors that caused you to create so much mess and clutter. You'll want to use The Game's technology to establish new habits that will keep your environment the way you truly want it to be. The following special rules for The Environment Game will sound familiar. They're things your parents or teachers may have told you. You know them, but the question is: Are you doing them?

When you use a cup or dish, don't leave it in the sink. Wash and dry it immediately and put it back in the cupboard. When you open a jar, put the lid back on and return it where it belongs. Simply stop making messes for yourself or others to clean up, and you'll eliminate some of the most time-wasting, unnecessary, and annoying tasks in your life. You'll also cut down on the frustration, agitation, and number of arguments that result from expecting and allowing your spouse or others to deal with your messes. So not only will you be creating the environment you want and need, you'll be going a long way toward having healthier and happier relationships with the people who have had to deal with your inconsiderate habits.

Give yourself points in The Environment Game every time you clean, and also when you return things where they belong. Rack up those points, and win a much more balanced and joyful life in 90 days.

Two special rules for the Environment Game are:
Clean as you go.
Return things how and where they belong.

It's Not My Job

When we mention the environment, most people think of the world out there where *others* aren't doing everything *they* should to take care of the planet. Just as with everything else in The Game, you'll discover that there is no *they;* there is only *you.* George Sutherland, one of our coaching program Gameplayers, inspired all of us with the change in his attitude toward the environment.

George says:

I already exercised one or two hours each day, so I didn't have to focus on this aspect of life during my Game. I did have to figure out which other areas of my life needed improvement so I could compete with my coaching program classmates and gather points for my Game.

The operative word in that line of thinking turned out to be gather. I decided that as I took my daily morning run along the Charles River in Boston, I'd pick up garbage that had been an eyesore to me. I'd always thought SOMEONE should do something about this litter. Of course, during The Game, that someone turned out to be me.

Along my running route, I picked up garbage and litter and gave myself one point for each piece I removed from the environment. I combined the motion of bending over to pick up trash with a stretching movement to make my workout more effective, since I'd always been a little lax about remembering to stretch before and after exercising.

I began to think of this new project as The Garbage Game, and it became a lot of fun. I eventually designated a "plastic bottle day," then a "Styrofoam day," a "glass day," a "yucky thing day," and finally, a "heavy and miscellaneous day." On the heavy day, I'd pick up castaway spare tires, old boards, and items that didn't fit into trash bags.

As I played The Garbage Game, a most interesting thing happened. Other runners got the idea that it wasn't necessary to endure this litter and start their days in such a disagreeable way. They started following my lead and picking up litter, also. Since my 90-day Game, I've formed the "Runners with a Garbage Problem" club.

Today, the Charles River is a much cleaner place.

By not waiting for other people to take responsibility for the environment, George made a difference. The fact that George is in this world has made it a better place. The fact that George set an example has caused other human beings to become better people. Can you say the same thing about yourself?

If you look at the many environments where people live in impoverished conditions, you'll see that on top of the poverty, they've victimized themselves by destroying or degrading where they live. While it's easy to blame others or the system for what our neighborhoods look like, the net result is that we get to live in our own trash.

Neighborhoods and communities have totally eradicated this problem by taking responsibility for their own environments and not expecting or waiting for others to clean it. Imagine a world in which, rather than people sitting isolated in their homes and watching television for three hours each night, everyone on the block skipped the sitcoms for 30 minutes, went outside, and cleaned up the streets in their neighborhood. There's nothing wrong with watching TV. The question is: Are you watching your environment with as much diligence?

Game-player Mary Wichmann says:

> *I've picked up clutter not only in my home, garage, car, and office, but in my neighborhood, the bathrooms in other people's homes, in hotel rooms, and even in the rest rooms on airplanes. I can no longer abandon a shopping cart in the parking lot. I return it to its proper place and get the additional benefits of some physical exercise along with a sense of completion.*

In addition to taking responsibility for cleaning the environment, you can add to your Environment Game any goals or principles you want to adopt from conservation, preservation, and planetary caretaking programs that align with your higher purpose and beliefs. You can also select design or space-arrangement methods that bring more beauty, calmness, harmony, and balance to your life, and make these systems part of your Environment Game.

> **A special rule for The Environment Game is:**
> ***Always leave places in a***
> ***better condition than how you found them.***

We added a corollary to this rule at the suggestion of a lady in our coaching program. She included, "Always put the toilet seat down before you leave the rest room."

ENVIRONMENT GAME EXERCISES
HOW DOES MY ENVIRONMENT REFLECT MY PURPOSE?

Walk around your living and work space, and cover every part of it. Look into those long-neglected closets, junk drawers, and all that stuff hidden in the garage or attic. Make a complete and honest assessment. Make lists of places in your environment that desperately need your attention and which don't reflect who you want to be as a person at all.

Which areas are most important in terms of functioning at maximum efficiency? It may be that the place you start working on first is in your purse or briefcase, if this is a constant source of disorganization and ineffectiveness.

Next, reshape your personal environment to go beyond neat and presentable into superefficient. Is your phone on your desk really in the most efficient place? Is your wastebasket big enough for all of the trash you seem to accumulate in a day? Make your environments reflect your higher purpose.

In addition to the activities with the special rules, do the following exercises if you decide to make The Environment

Game one of the three to five aspects of life you want to improve in 90 days. Also, design The Environment Game by using The Game's basic elements described in Part III of this book: goals, To-Be and Not-To-Be lists, points, prizes, rules, Before-and-After Displays, essays, skills, rewards, consequences, deadlines, partners, and coaches.

If you're adopting a special program or system for The Environment Game, give yourself points for using it. An example of a consequence for not achieving goals in The Environment Game would be if you make a commitment to your Game partner that if you don't get your house in order, you'll come over and clean theirs. Or if you don't keep your commitments and achieve your environmental goals, you'll take a broom and sweep the streets in your entire neighborhood. Refer to **TheGameInteractive.com** Website for more ideas and coaching specifically targeted to improving your performance in The Environment Game.

Use the information in Part I of this book in the chapters "Time," "Structure," "Affinity," "Community," and "Purpose" to balance and coordinate The Environment Game with your overall Game plan.

✳ ✳ ✳

In the next chapter, you're going to learn a whole new way of looking at education. You'll see that it is an ongoing and tremendously exciting process that continues throughout your entire life.

✳ ✳ ✳

✶ CHAPTER 14 ✶

Your Education

So you thought your education was over. You're either in the midst of paying off, or have already paid off, those student loans. You've graduated or are about to. No more schoolrooms; no more books. No more education, right?

Or you're a student and your job is to pay attention in school, do your assignments, study hard, and make good grades. That's learning. That's education, right?

Or you consider yourself to be a lifelong learner. You read, study, research, and keep up on current events. You're the person who bought the set of encyclopedias and actually uses them. You're an educated person, right?

The Education Game is going to utilize a whole different approach to improving your base of knowledge. My father used to say that if a person lived to be 100, he was simply living to be 10 years old . . . ten times over. Basically, a lot of people settled into their lifelong learning styles and patterns about midway through elementary school. From that point on, they contracted and declined, rather than expanding on their ability to learn.

I'm going to show you that you don't have to be one of those people who is growing smaller due to a lack of true education. You can continue to be a student of life until the day you die.

Observing You

In The Education Game, you're going to start thinking about those things that you usually focus your attention on. After you've determined what your attention-grabbers are, you'll be able to expand, shift, and focus your attention wherever you want. *Focusing your attention* is the key to expanding your ability to learn.

This Game isn't designed to tell you what subjects to study. That's up to you. Instead, you'll inquire into the nature of your own thinking to discover your view of the world and how you relate to others. By playing The Education Game, you'll uncover aspects of yourself that have been hidden.

After you've applied the techniques you'll read about in this chapter, you'll be able to embrace just about any subject. The ability to understand how you're focusing your attention will give you the freedom to study anything you choose. In The Education Game, you'll open your eyes to see the kind of world you've constructed and what limits you've placed on yourself.

Life As Coaching

Playing The Education Game will show you how to take the experiences of life and turn them into opportunities for learning and coaching. As you analyze what's going on in your own thought processes and how you relate to others—particularly whatever might be causing you difficulty—you'll realize that the lessons life is presenting you are needed for your "advanced" education. You'll truly appreciate the old adage that *everything happens for a reason.*

Game-player Steve Powilatis shares his experiences playing The Education Game.

Steve says:

> *I began to see things, not as "broken" or "right" or "wrong," but merely as they are. Instead of categorizing my experiences into having to get somewhere or be something, I see every experience as a miracle, perfect just as it is.*
>
> *After playing The Game for 90 days, my mind is quieted enough so that I can hear the world, and it sounds just fine. Rain is a wonderful experience. There's nothing wrong with getting wet; wet can be an amazing experience if I allow myself to enjoy it.*
>
> *I used to get caught up in the "should-be's," as in "I should be dry and comfortable." This is true, but I was taking a class in Boston and I walked home in the rain. Instead of fighting it, I resolved to get really wet, to feel the rain, and just be with it. I noticed people around me running and trying desperately to escape. I thought that this was like life, where we're always trying to avoid where we are and who we are. If we could just resolve that we're going to get wet, we'd find that at this moment it's the perfect way to be.*

**A special rule for The Game, in general,
and The Education Game, in particular is:
*Take life as coaching.***

Conflict As Coaching

What do you think causes conflict?

There's a story that floats around in theater circles about a director who was teaching a group of actors how to create conflict on the stage. He'd present a situation and ask two actors to improvise the scene with a great deal of conflict in it. One day, when he couldn't get the actors to be as dramatic as he wanted, this director tried a different tactic. He took each of the actors aside and whispered instructions to them separately. Then the two actors returned to the stage and played the scene with the desired dramatic conflict. Afterwards, the director analyzed the scenes and compared the first try, when the actors were placid and undramatic, with the second scene, when they'd come alive with conflict. One of the class members asked the director how he'd created a higher level of conflict with the actors. He said, "I told each of them something completely different about the scene."

This is what happens when relationships have conflict. The two people each think the scene they're playing is about something different. Each person believes he or she is the central character. They've forgotten that their relationship should be the most important character on stage.

Did you know that you can study how you relate to others? You can use conflict in relationships as another opportunity for learning and growing.

Try this activity throughout your 90 days of The Education Game. You're going to really study what it's like to be *you* when you're having a conflict or argument with someone. This exercise allows you to stop and shift your attention to learning what conflict is teaching you.

Do this by switching roles with someone when you're having a disagreement (or shortly afterwards). With all your might, the two of you should argue each other's points of view. This will place you in a seat where you're facing yourself in the mirror. You'll observe what it's like to experience *you*. By shifting your attention to the other person's viewpoint, you'll see how you're relating to another human being. After you've done this activity and seen yourself more clearly, you'll have the freedom to make different choices in how you relate to others.

I learned this lesson of shifting my attention to the other person's viewpoint early in my relationship with my daughter, Georgia. When she was three years old, we were walking down some icy stairs in New York City. Since Georgia was so small,

I asked her to hold my hand because I didn't want her to fall. But even at this young age, Georgia was very independent. For her, accepting my hand meant that she'd have to admit she was a weak and helpless little girl. This is something she absolutely refused to do, and she made her position clear by throwing a temper tantrum and telling me in no uncertain terms that she'd walk down the stairs by herself.

I could feel anger rising in me. But suddenly I stopped what I was feeling and remembered to shift my attention to *her* viewpoint. This brought me to a whole new level of understanding. I looked at my daughter and said, "Georgia, the stairs are slippery. Could you help me keep my balance by holding my hand?"

With that change in her viewpoint, Georgia no longer believed that I was belittling her, so she immediately took my hand, grabbed the banister, and walked down the stairs. We had avoided conflict by shifting our attention to each other's points of view.

A special rule for the Education Game is:
Take conflict as coaching.

What Draws Your Attention?

To facilitate learning how *you* learn, I'd like you to become an observer of your own life and thought patterns. It's as if you're going to be outside yourself, looking at how you relate to the world around you. This is how you'll begin to understand where you're placing your attention. The more attentive and present you are to each moment, person, and activity, the greater you'll increase your ability to learn from life.

Walk into a gathering of people and observe how you don't immediately notice everyone in the room. Just stroll around and see which people catch your attention and most clearly come into view. Then, observe which ones have remained in the background for you. These background people are a reflection of your worldview. They aren't important to you and don't rate getting your attention right away. They may be so different from you that you consider them to be inferior, so you don't notice them. Or they may be so much like you that you don't see them any more than you'd look at your own arm or foot.

Analyze why your attention was drawn to some people in that room and not others. This will help you figure out what people and aspects of the world around you have been slipping off your radar screen for years. Now you have the freedom to shift your attention to a broader, more expansive view. As if you were playing chess or checkers, you can move figures from the background to the foreground of your attention. This exercise isn't leading you to any "right" conclusions, but it's opening a whole new process of seeing the world around you.

Use this exercise frequently during your Education Game. Observe how your attention shifts over 90 days. What new colors and shades of color are you seeing in your world that you didn't even know were there three months ago? What possibilities are people you don't ordinarily notice bringing with them? As your attention shifts, you're broadening your worldview and becoming a more expansive and caring human being, because attention and love grow hand-in-hand.

When one of **TheCoachingProgram.com** clients did this exercise, she observed that whenever she walked into a room, she only noticed whomever she considered to be exceptionally smart or excessively dumb. This practice meant that about 99 percent of the people in the room remained invisible to her. My client realized that her attention was a reflection of concern over her own intelligence, which she bolsters by having three advanced college degrees. Placing her attention only on the level of intelligence she perceived in others kept her from relating to most people. This exercise helped her discover that she'd been missing a lot!

People who haven't drawn your attention also signal you

about qualities and characteristics you're ignoring in yourself. These can be habits that annoy others but are your blind spots. When you analyze the people you didn't notice in the room at first, look at what they're doing, how they're dressed, what they're saying, and their speech patterns. Do they speak loudly, fast, or with a lot of gestures? Are the people they're talking to trying to get away from them or looking bored or agitated?

Have fun studying these mirrors of yourself and using what you're learning to have better relationships—or at least less boring cocktail party conversations.

A special rule for The Education Game is:
Learn about yourself by noticing who and what does or doesn't draw your attention.

Learning How to Refocus Your Attention

Another assignment for The Education Game is to observe how your attention drifts from what you're doing in the present to daydreaming. This might happen while someone is talking to you and you're supposed to be listening, but instead, you're chattering internally to yourself.

Any activity can be a catalyst for daydreaming. Let's say you're washing the dishes and your mind drifts off aimlessly. When you notice this, rather than criticize yourself or examine the contents of your thoughts, gently bring yourself back to the present moment. This teaches your mind to focus attention more fully on whatever you're doing, and increases your capacity for learning. The more attention you give to something, the more you learn from it.

In any activity you're doing, return to the present by using your senses—sight, hearing, touch, taste, and smell. In the dishwashing scenario, hear the kitchen sounds, the sloshing of water, and the birds singing outside your window. Feel the soap suds on your hands and arms. Smell the scent of the dishwashing detergent. Look at the dishes carefully and give your full attention to scrubbing them until they shine, rinsing the soap film away and drying them carefully. This is how you train your mind to connect to the present.

Practice using your five senses to return to the present when you find yourself driving and aimlessly daydreaming. Turn your attention to the full range of sensations and experiences that go with driving. Feel the road beneath you, the smells inside and outside your car, the flashes of color on the road, and the sounds of traffic. See how long you can drive while bringing your attention back to the actual experience of driving.

Also notice which activities are more likely than others to cause you to daydream. These may be ones you're resisting, so you end up getting caught inside your own mind, trying to avoid them.

Use the exercise I've described above every day for 90 days when you catch yourself daydreaming. The results will absolutely amaze you as you realize how much you've been missing. If you don't take the time to watch how you're losing focus, you'll lose the freedom to choose what you want to place your attention on.

A special rule for The Education Game is:
Notice what triggers daydreaming,
and use your five senses to return to the present.

Studying Your Thoughts

To increase your skill at learning how you learn, you're going to study your thoughts and assumptions. We all have the tendency at times to indulge in black-and-white thinking and to make judgments based on prejudices.

A client from our coaching program has very strong religious beliefs, and he used to teach his daughter that interracial dating was wrong. This was (literally) his black-and-white attitude. After he began playing The Education Game and using some of the exercises in it, he started observing his thinking and assumptions. He realized that he was not seeing shades of gray on the subject of interracial dating. Now he teaches his daughter that interracial dating has consequences, just as same-race dating does. When you date outside of your race, you have to be prepared to deal with these consequences. By observing his thought patterns, this man was able to check whether or not his assumptions were always true, or if he needed to modify them.

For most of us, our minds are lazy and resist taking a look at our underlying assumptions. To learn how you learn, ask yourself: *What do I believe about my beliefs?* This will help you inquire into the nature of how you understand the world. Do you believe all clouds have silver linings? Or is this something you've embraced to help you become more optimistic? What exactly do you feel about the beliefs that have solidified like blocks of concrete in your mind? Do you consider yourself to be right, and anyone who believes something different from you to be wrong? Are you indulging in black-and-white thinking?

A special rule for The Education Game is:
Reduce black-and-white thinking; explore shades of gray.

Learning What It's Like to Experience You

When you're in an argument with someone, you're usually only looking at things from your own point of view. Your attention is only on your own thoughts and feelings. But what if you could see yourself as others see and experience you? Would this help you become a better listener and learner? I think so.

One of the greatest opportunities for learning how to shift your attention is when you're involved in a conflict. And your Game-partner is one of the most important people to practice shifting attention with. This is where you'll have the chance to work with someone who is studying the same things you are and has been practicing the exercise of Refreshing.

Try shifting your attention the next time you're in an argument with someone. Ask the other person's permission for you to clear your mind so you can be more present to their needs. Then, Refresh and watch how your mind focuses more easily as your emotions slow down. From that quieter space, inform the person that you'd like to know how you're coming across in this argument. Ask if the other person would help by repeating what you've been saying and pretend to be you. Then switch roles and do the same for him or her. This can be the source of much laughter as you get to see, when your mind is no longer blurred by conflict, how different you're being perceived from the way you intended to come across. Discuss these differences with the other person, and resolve your conflicts with greater compassion.

A special rule for The Education Game is:
*Shift your attention during conflict to learn
how the other person is experiencing you.*

Learning More about Learning

As with all the other Games in Part II of this book, you can use the principles and ideas from any methods or techniques that align with your higher purpose and fit in with your belief system. Plug into The Education Game any books and audiocassettes about how people learn, and put their suggestions on your To-Be and Not-To-Be lists. Give yourself points for following their suggestions for changing your habits and behaviors.

I especially encourage you to explore information on how memory works during The Education Game. What you remember is directly related to your attention, so improving your memory also helps you focus and expand your ability to learn in every other aspect of life.

Use the techniques I introduce in Part III of this book to teach yourself how to increase the rate at which you read. Again, you'll be furthering your education with respect to how attention and daydreaming work against each other.

After you've mastered their fundamental principles, all the systems of thought you'll explore in The Education Game offer ways for you to become more effective at anything you want to do. They'll help you observe how you learn, and give you choices for relating to other human beings.

EDUCATION GAME EXERCISES

Do the activities described with the special rules above if you decide to make The Education Game one of the three to five aspects of life you want to improve in 90 days. Also, design The Education Game by using The Game's basic elements described in Part III of this book: goals, To-Be and Not-To-Be lists, points, prizes, rules, Before-and-After Displays, essays, skills, rewards, consequences, deadlines, partners, and coaches.

If you're adopting a special program or system for The Education Game, give yourself points for using it. An example of a consequence for not achieving goals in The Education Game would be that if you don't keep your education commitments to yourself, create your own "dunce cap" and wear it around the house and at work. Instead of saying "dunce," your cap should say, "I don't pay enough attention." Refer to **TheGameInteractive.com** Website for more ideas and coaching specifically targeted to improving your performance in The Education Game.

Use the information in Part I of this book in the chapters "Time," "Structure," "Affinity," "Community," and "Purpose" to balance and coordinate The Education Game with your overall Game plan.

✳ ✳ ✳

Your family members are probably the most important people in your life, yet when you think about how much time and effort you put into relationships with them, you may feel a little regretful. In the next chapter, you'll start turning those regrets into sources of satisfaction and peace.

✳ ✳ ✳

Chapter 15

Your Family

W hat could be more fun and ideal for a family than to learn how to love and support each other and handle conflicts by playing The Game together?

In The Family Game, you'll have the opportunity to lead by example or to invite your family members to play along with you. You'll be able to use The Game's technology of setting goals, scoring points, having deadlines, thinking of funny consequences, getting rewards, and uniting with other communities. You'll turn conflicts, which used to divide your family, into optimum experiences for learning and growth.

As with the other special games in this book, you can use whatever systems or philosophies align with your higher purpose and fit in with your belief system to strengthen the love within your family. This may include setting goals and giving yourself points for attending family therapy sessions, and keeping the commitments for improvement that you make to one another during counseling.

You may be the one who has to take the initiative in The Family Game. As you decide which aspects of your life you most want to improve and start playing those Games for 90 days, it's likely that family members will want to support and join you. Instead of complaining about the terrible things family members are doing, you'll be taking responsibility for your behavior in the home. Your spouse and children will become the beneficiaries of the changes you're making inside yourself.

Game-players from our coaching program have found that family activities they'd neglected, such as reading bedtime stories to their children and being more attentive to their spouses, led to deep and honest conversation. Family members of Game-players often expressed admiration and appreciation for the positive changes they were witnessing.

A **CoachingProgram.com** client says that while driving his daughter to school one day while he was playing The Game, she said, "I think you and Mom are doing a pretty good job of raising me." High praise from a teenager.

Bill Meyer noticed his improvement as a parent and the positive impact on his family life.

He says:

> I think certain things I was doing in The Game helped me see my kids more for who they are and less for some imagined "what they ought to be." Instead of saying, "Do it now because I said so!" as I used to, I've become much more understanding and compassionate. That has helped everyone in my family.
>
> I made it part of my Game to sing my daughter awake every morning. Now she gets out of bed very fast if I threaten to sing to her again.

It's a Game. It's fun. It's a pleasure to play it with your family. And it's tremendously enjoyable to watch the transformations in yourself and those you love.

A special rule for The Family Game is:
Lead by example.

When to Play The Family Game

You know my philosophy about when to play The Game. You've delayed and put off winning your life until "someday" and "later" long enough. *Now* is the best time to start The Family Game.

Let's say you're a newly formed family and you're about to become a parent. Why not put all your preparations for the baby into the Game technology? Set up your structures, affinity, and community, and select your Game partner and coaches to help you get ready for this new experience. Have these in place when you come home from the hospital instead of coping with first-time parenthood in isolation.

What if your children are teenagers? Will they think that playing The Family Game isn't cool? Don't they already have fun when they play video games and sports? Design your Family Game together, and turn things that have been bones of contention in the past into ways for scoring points and winning special prizes. Register to play The Family Game on **TheGame-Interactive.com's** Website or by mailing in the registration form in Chapter 28. As a family, play The Game to win the grand cash prizes.

What if you're not the "traditional" family? Should you wait to start The Family Game until you have an "ideal" family? In today's world, families are created in many ways. Playing The Family Game can strengthen the bonds of love, unity, and support in any kind of extended family that people form— families of friends, grandparent and grandchildren families, even families comprised of roommates and fellow students in college dormitories. You can use The Game's technology and the special Family Game rules to break through any limitations you may have accepted with respect to what families are, can be, or should do.

A special rule for The Family Game is:
Don't wait; start The Family Game right away.

The Family's Higher Purpose

In The Family Game, one of the most important first steps is for the entire family to create a statement of higher purpose. Then, as a strong unit, the family can commit to it. With the higher purpose in view, design goals for the family's To-Be and Not-To-Be list, and decide what behaviors and habits will be eligible for making or taking away points. Remember that there is no self-criticism in The Game. For The Family Game, you'll lose points for criticizing other family members. By articulating the family's higher purpose, each member now has a focus for producing results and aligning behind the meaning this family has for each other, for their neighborhood, for their community, and for the world.

Because my ex-wife, Christine, and I now have a brother/sister-type relationship, we wanted to make sure that regardless of what changes went on in our lives, we kept our family intact—unlike many families that we'd seen go through divorce. One of the things we stated in the Kelley family's higher purpose statement is that "the family is indivisible and indestructible. It can be added to but never taken away from." We've let our friends and the people Christine and I date know up front that our family continues to be united in a higher purpose, and we invite them into a constellation that is composed of my ex-wife, my daughter, and me. Due to this type of clarity, Christine and I have been able to be honest with people early in our relationships with them. If they're not comfortable with the way Christine and I still interact, even though we're divorced, the people we date can let us know right away.

With all of your family members, take a look at what kind of legacy all of you want to leave for the future. Your higher purpose should be a statement that reflects what generations 100 years from now will say about your family unit.

A special rule for The Family Game is:
Design and agree upon your family's higher purpose.

Handling Family Conflict As a Game

When you try to alter a family member's conduct by domination, coercion, or manipulation, you only succeed in stopping or forestalling the behavior. You haven't taught the individual how to control their own habits. Instead, you've merely succeeded in temporarily controlling them.

If you want to teach family members to control their own behavior and become more mature, help them set up a structure, affinity, and community for the new habits they need to acquire. Children love to play games. Instead of lecturing and punishing them, transform whatever is a source of conflict or agitation in your family by using The Game's technology. In this way, the things that have divided you can become catalysts for having fun, learning together, and making family life a coaching experience.

For example, a typical family conflict revolves around children not making their beds or keeping their clothes and toys orderly. With The Family Game, you now have the option of making these irritating habits into a Game. You don't need to nag at your children or throw your hands up in despair and keep their bedroom doors closed. After your family has decided what its higher purpose is, it becomes very clear what does and doesn't move it forward. With your To-Be and Not-To-Be lists, Before-and-After Displays, point systems, prizes, and funny consequences, children can score points for keeping their room clean. By playing The Family Game, you'll be giving them your time and attention in positive ways rather than through the negative habits of scolding and punishing.

One of the most wasteful things about most family conflicts is that they're usually about something in the past that no one can change. Arguing over who was "right" and who was "wrong" is about as useful as spitting into a hurricane. Instead, use a more thoughtful approach to head off problems while you plan for playing The Family Game. Without blame or anger, distinguish the usual subjects and sources of family conflict. Ask each member to suggest countermeasures, and put them into The Family Game.

A special rule for The Family Game is:
Use The Game to transform conflict into
opportunities for learning and bonding as a family.

Returning to Mend Family Fences

Some people in our coaching program made mending family relationships part of their Game. They found that seeking and granting forgiveness and making amends helped them become the compassionate and responsible human beings they wanted to be. Game-player Greg Kadet shares his experience of taking his longtime relationship with family members to a new level of understanding.

Greg says:

I'm very much a family person. I'm sensitive to the issues of being the baby of my family. I always needed and wanted a lot of attention.

I always found relationships with my mother to be difficult. It hurt that my mother had never ever told me that she loved me or was proud of me. I interpreted her lack of expression as meaning that there must be something wrong with me. Perhaps, I thought, I just wasn't good enough for her to love. I grew into adulthood with feelings that I'd never be good enough. Deep down I believed that nothing in my life would ever be successful.

Since playing The Game, I've started having honest conversations with my mother. We've gone from our usual habit of yelling at each other through 95 percent of our discussions to spending only 5 percent of our time in conflict. After I told my mother that it bothered me that she'd never expressed her love for me, she told me for the first time in 28 years that she does love me. And I told her I loved her.

As our conversations have continued, we've put years of frustration out on the table and discussed past hurts and misunderstandings.

I feel that my biggest accomplishment as a member of my family is not to give in to urges to lash out at my mother. I no longer try to fight with her in order to prove that I'm right and she's wrong. I don't have the need to direct my mother in any way. I'm more trusting of her. Today we have a very enjoyable relationship. I view my mother with more compassion and understanding, as well as with a non-manipulative attitude.

My family went through tremendous healing while I played The Game for the first time. I'd decided that I needed to overcome the problems that poor family relationships had caused inside of me. This was one of the hardest things I ever did. But I needed to get over the past so our family could relate to each other in the here-and-now.

Brooke, the woman I'm about to marry, is extremely pleased that I've dealt with these big issues before we start our lives together. She sees that the more I mend relationships with my family, the better of a husband I will be to her.

Sit down with your family members and make a list of relatives whom you no longer communicate with. This list might include "the black sheep of the family" whom everyone shuns. Call these relatives during your 90-day Family Game to ask how they're doing. Let them know that if they ever need you, you're all still family, no matter what. Although it might be difficult to pick up the phone and make that initial call, it will be well worth it in the end.

> **A special rule for The Family Game is:**
> *Make amends, and take responsibility*
> *for repairing family relationships.*

Start The Family Game with Enthusiasm

It's a good idea to start playing The Family Game by choosing something as a goal that family members can enthusiastically agree to accomplish together. In this way, you'll learn how to do something fun together, and it will prepare you for eventually using The Game's technology to tackle family conflicts.

A really great goal for a family to pursue together is to save money for something you all really want. One of the women in our coaching classes says that her children were always asking her to take them to Disneyland. Her inability to find the time and money for this kind of vacation had become the source of much consternation.

She decided to make the goal of vacationing at Disneyland part of The Family Game. She told her children, "You come up with the money for this vacation, and I'll find the time to get off work and take you." They picked a deadline and divided up the number of days until then. They came up with a dollar amount that each child would put into a family piggy bank every day to save money for this prize.

Within several months, the children had raised enough money for their dream vacation. Something that had been the source of family problems and a lot of complaining had turned into a constructive opportunity for this mother and her children to achieve a goal together. The other great thing about this Family Game was that the children learned the value of saving money for something they wanted instead of expecting Mom to give them a handout.

Other possibilities for family goals could be hosting a family reunion or get-together. Rather than doing it alone, enlist the entire family's help in making invitations, e-mailing people, calling relatives no one has heard from in a while, and putting together an all-around wonderful event.

A special rule for The Family Game is:
*Establish a goal that everyone
in your family is enthusiastic about.*

FAMILY GAME EXERCISES

Use the activities with the special rules above if you decide to make The Family Game one of the three to five aspects of life you want to improve in 90 days. Also, design The Family Game by using The Game's basic elements described in Part III of this book: goals, To-Be and Not-To-Be lists, points, prizes, rules, Before-and-After Display, essays, skills, rewards, consequences, deadlines, partners, and coaches. Add any goals or principles you're adopting from family therapy or special systems or philosophies to your Family Game.

Avoid making household chores a consequence for The Family Game, since chores are a great opportunity to work together as a family. Instead, have each family member come up with a consequence of their own that they'd be willing to pay but hope will never happen. A consequence my daughter Georgia and I made when we played The Game was that if I scored fewer points than she did, I had to wait on her hand and foot for a day.

An example of a consequence for the entire family not achieving their goals could be that you'll all go to the local ice cream parlor, sit together, and watch other people eat ice cream as you just drink water. Refer to **TheGame-**

Interactive.com Website for more ideas and coaching specifically targeted to improving your performance in The Family Game.

Use the information in Part I of this book in the chapters "Time," "Structure," "Affinity," "Community," and "Purpose" to balance and coordinate The Family Game with your overall Game plan.

* * *

We spend the major portion of our days working either at home, in an office, or at a work site of some kind. In the next chapter, you're going to learn how to start having much more fun with work while becoming more productive than you've ever been.

* * *

⋆ CHAPTER 16 ⋆

Your Work

I s work really only about work? Is it only about how many promotions you can get or the amount of money you earn? Is it about the friends you make or the relief from boredom that comes from having something to do and somewhere to go every day? Is work about finding the right career or climbing down from the corporate ladder to chuck it all? Is work about being on or off the "Mommy" or the "fast" tracks?

If you choose to play The Work Game for 90 days, you'll discover that the answer to all of those questions is yes, no, and maybe. That's because whatever you do for work makes absolutely no difference at all. Work, as you'll soon see, is highly overrated as a means for defining who you are and what your value is to others, to yourself, to the world. As Dr. Wayne Dyer says, "If what you do is what you are, then when you don't, you aren't."

One of the primary excuses people give for not being effective or happy with their work is that they're waiting for the right job—just like they're waiting for the right relationship, the right life, and the right body. Then they'll be happy and take action to accomplish their goals. Here's what they don't see. They've been practicing absentmindedness. Whatever skills they're not developing, whatever talents they're waiting to cultivate, whatever practices they're not observing . . . is what they'll bring to the next job. And guess what? That job won't be right either, because all this time they've been learning how to be ineffective.

Paying Attention to Your Work

If you've ever wondered what gets your attention the most, you might want to try watching a cat. Anyone who has a cat for a pet knows that these little creatures will sit, stand, or walk all over whatever is most drawing their human's attention (such as a book, newspaper, or even the evening meal!).

In The Work Game, you're going to annoy your cat by paying full attention to whatever job you're currently doing. When you focus fully on the job in front of you, you'll grow to love that work.

If you get overwhelmed by the idea that you need a "right" career, you'll miss the chance to love what you're doing *now*. The surest way to have no career satisfaction is to conserve your energy and talents for that career of a lifetime that's out there somewhere in the future.

When you pay profound attention to each task and become present to exactly what you're doing in the moment, this creates a peace of mind like nothing you've ever experienced. You'll begin to observe the work happening effortlessly. This is totally different from working while your mind is daydreaming.

Try it. Right now. Place your complete focus and attention on reading this book. Observe your eyes moving across the page, feel the touch of paper on your fingertips, and hear the sound of the page turning. Become present to the sensations you're having as ideas occur and as you and I, although miles apart, communicate with each other and embark on the journey of this book together. Isn't this level of presence much more satisfying than how you ordinarily approach your job?

Carpentry is a great example of a task you can become profoundly present to doing. Rather than thinking about having to lift the hammer up and pound it down, if you're paying attention to the hammer hitting the nail squarely, broadening the stroke each time, and watching the nail go down into the board, how likely is it that you're going to hit your thumb with that hammer? By focusing attention on the work, it becomes a wondrous activity, as opposed to requiring a lot of effort or becoming a possible source of injury and pain.

How likely is it that doing your work absentmindedly will encourage your boss to give you an even more challenging job? If you're showing how untalented or unhappy you are with what you're doing now, why would you be given something better to do? Many people worry about the possibility of being downsized when, if they put effort and energy into increasing their attention on the work, their level of productivity would make them irreplaceable.

A special rule for The Work Game is:
Become fully present to whatever
work you're currently doing.

Do You Have a Calling?

One of the most important things you can do to increase your level of satisfaction with work is to become as productive as possible. While in the process of becoming more productive, you may start hearing the still, small voice telling you what your calling is in life. Because of the skills you've developed through attentiveness, you'll be able to pursue this calling with vigor and confidence. You may not even have to work for a different company or become an entrepreneur (unless this is what you want to do) to pursue your calling. Even in the most established corporations today, if you have an incredibly profitable and productive idea, you can create your own role. While playing The Work Game, you'll become a leader instead of simply waiting for someone else to determine your future.

One of the things that makes finding a career or calling so challenging is that you're probably the last person to know what you should be doing. This is why it helps to ask the people around you if they can see what your unique gifts are. Ask them: "What do you think I do well without much thought or effort?" These natural gifts are things you probably haven't considered as leading to work possibilities or your calling. You do them so effortlessly (and absentmindedly) that you're not present to them.

For example, it's not difficult to understand why I'm a motivational speaker. I love to talk. Often people come up to me after my speeches and say, "I want to be a motivational speaker."

I ask them, "Are you already speaking?" Usually they reply with some long story about why they're not doing this kind of work yet. Then I respond by saying, "I can tell when someone is a motivational speaker, because they're speaking. You couldn't pay them to shut up. They're not waiting for the chance to speak. It's who they are and what they do."

After you've asked the people in your life to tell you what your unique gifts are, then expand your thinking by also asking them what kinds of jobs they know of that have a need for your skills. Research that is done with the help of others opens you to a world of new paradigms and creates an unlimited universe of possibilities.

A special rule for playing The Work Game is:
*Ask your community to help you find
work that uses your natural gifts and talents.*

Getting Paid for Your Calling

When you pursue your natural gifts and talents, people will want to pay you for your services. This is how we get our Michael Jordans and Tiger Woods. They love the game, and people love to watch them. For them, their natural gifts are almost transparent.

"Doc" Kettelhut was one of the original master coaches for **TheCoachingProgram.com.** He tells how he created his calling by doing what he loves.

Dr. Kettelhut says:

> *What I love to do is have conversations in which people discover something about themselves or life that they didn't know was possible. So all through my education and previous jobs, I found myself having those kinds of conversations. I didn't know I was ever going to make a career out of this. If I looked at the list of careers in my high school or college directory, I wouldn't have found a category for what I currently do. But I kept doing it, and now people pay me for personal coaching. When I was getting my education, this wasn't even heard of as a career choice. I was able to create the work by my persistence in doing what I love.*

One of the great advantages to operating as Dr. Kettelhut does is that when you're doing what you love, payment is irrelevant. In fact, many people who wind up with incredibly satisfying jobs were volunteers in that particular area first. Yet, the strangest thing happens. People who do what they love and would do it for free tend to get paid the most.

Game-player Allen Staples says that a fellow stockbroker in his company asked for his help on her biggest account. Through no fault of her own, she'd lost her second largest account, and it had been devastating to her. Because playing The Game was causing Allen to look at life differently, he decided to help this co-worker save the account—not as a business partner, but out of friendship. He asked for nothing in return and didn't expect to profit in any way from assisting her. Even though this hadn't been Allen's intention, when their work together proved successful, his co-worker voluntarily split her commissions from the account with Allen. He'd done the work out of love and concern, but life just couldn't resist rewarding him.

A special rule of The Work Game is:
Do what you love whether you get paid for it or not.

The Work of Leadership

When you place your full attention and love on whatever you're doing, you'll find yourself becoming busier than ever. You may have already noticed that more work always goes to the busiest person. When you're showing maximum productivity in the job you currently do, you're not focused on promotion; instead, your attention is on the work at hand. This creates a loving relationship between you and the work. Others notice how well you do your job. Without any extra effort or manipulation, greater opportunities come your way.

The key to getting promoted, then, is paying so much attention to loving what you do that it doesn't *matter* if you get promoted. Your productivity and love will attract opportunities, and you can choose to accept them or not. Playing The Work Game gives you the freedom to make these choices instead of merely working for "The Man" and being chained to the process of earning a living instead of earning a life.

Another way to become a leader at work is to take responsibility for transforming your environment and uplifting it. If you're like most people, you think that going to work means sitting or standing at a certain location and doing a specific activity. Often we fail to look around and recognize that we're spending at least eight hours a day—the longest period of time we're conscious—being with co-workers. This is a community you definitely want to cultivate. If you're working alone at home, your co-workers might be the people you're interacting with over the phone or on the Internet.

How many of us see it as our responsibility to contribute to these people's lives? Or to create an environment where they feel a team spirit? How often do we wait for someone else to do this kind of teambuilding?

One of the practices our coaching clients have done is to throw birthday parties for their co-workers as a way of giving personal service and building a working community. This is a simple activity, but it makes the work environment more enjoyable and cohesive.

> **A special rule for playing The Work Game is:**
> *Transform your job into a*
> *work environment that you and others love.*

The Benefits of Becoming a Failure

Dr. Laurence J. Peter's book *The Peter Principle* (Amereon Ltd., reprint edition, October 2000) became a classic by showing how employees get promoted to the level of their incompetence. People all over the world were nodding their heads and agreeing that the problem with American business was that people were being pushed into failure.

Playing The Work Game will show you a whole different way to view failure. To expand your abilities, you'll need to *push* yourself to fail. This is similar to lifting weights when the most difficult and final repetitions of a movement create the greatest muscle growth.

If you find that you're bored at work and daydreaming all the time, then your work isn't challenging you enough. George

Thompson says that when he played The Game and decided that he wanted to live his work life more in line with his higher purpose, he challenged himself more. Instead of setting the goal of making a million dollars himself, he switched to the aim of teaching *others* how to make a million dollars. George had previously written a 20-page workbook to present his unique principles. During his 90-day Game, he published this material as a 104-page book with an accompanying audiocassette.

George increased his challenges to himself and risked failure. He started doing much more public speaking, taking his book and tape to new audiences. He'd changed his focus to affecting humanity by helping people become more prosperous. This prompted him to become a better listener as well as a speaker. Before long, he had more speaking requests than he could handle, he'd doubled his business, and he'd received glowing testimonials for his book. He'd pushed himself into areas where he could have failed, and he found great personal satisfaction in doing so.

Beyond Failure

Here's something to remember about the prospect of failure: *If you're not failing, you're not playing The Game. If you're not failing, you're not winning your life.* Creating a way to fail means that you challenge yourself beyond the secure ways in which you've always set things up. You take on more responsibility or do new tasks. This is how you learn and expand. This is how you live a much more exhilarating life.

In **TheCoachingProgram.com**, we encourage clients to take on extraordinary goals, projects, and tasks that they wouldn't think are possible or that they've given no thought to doing until now. Immediately, they fear failure—as well they should. Failure is just as much a part of achieving an extraordinary goal as success is. I've seen in my clients and myself that the larger the goal, the greater the expansion. While we often don't achieve our goals, we far exceed our limitations. This is a most important and valuable process and outcome. By setting ourselves up for failure and reaching beyond our grasp, we open a space to achieve the impossible. By stretching to fail, you're moving yourself forward. Your goals are so expansive and "unrealistic" that you have to come up with a plan, the money, and creativity to achieve them

Think of any sport. There's no game if there's no failure. Players would be sitting on the field sucking their thumbs without the possibility of failure. Your inability to perfectly achieve all your goals in The Game is an indication that you're playing wholeheartedly. If you're failing, you're in The Game; you're not complaining, whining, waiting, or frozen into inaction. You're moving forward. The terrific part of failing while you play The Game is that now you have structure, affinity, and community to support you as you keep pushing yourself beyond where you ever thought you could go.

Most people fail to fail. They're resigned to not even trying and don't get engaged in life or their work. In the process of playing The Game, I want you to allow your goals to be so expansive that failure is *guaranteed*. In the face of failure, you will create and explore levels of success that you never could have imagined.

A special rule for The Work Game is:
Create work goals that will lead to failure and beyond.

Your Company's Higher Purpose

In his book, *Faster Than the Speed of Change* (Akiba Press, 2000), executive coach, futurist, and entrepreneur Paul Lemberg advises companies to make business a game. He says, "Games have players, teams, rules, and fun."

After you've read this book and have decided which aspects of your life you want to improve most, also consider proposing that your entire company play The Game.

As a business, design a higher purpose. This could be quite different from most company's mission statements, although they may contain elements of a higher purpose in them. Can you imagine working at a place where every day, a group of people are dedicated to making contributions that give service to all life?

Next, set up businesswide goals, points, rewards, consequences, and deadlines using The Game's technology and aligning behind the company's higher purpose. If you want to make The Game really fun, get some other companies to also play The Game and compete with yours for prizes.

When any business starts, it has some initial calling. It sees a human need and starts providing a service for fulfilling that need. But the spark is often lost as the founders move on and the business grows. Now, as an organization, your company can refocus and reacquaint the entire company with the business's higher purpose. Employees and managers who are focused on the company's purpose will be able to communicate the business's higher calling more clearly to customers, vendors, and suppliers. The commitment for fulfilling this higher purpose will grow exponentially.

As a company, the organization can offer special prizes and incentives to anyone who goes the extra mile toward fulfilling the firm's higher purpose or achieving the goals aligned with it. Your company can also encourage community service through donations and volunteerism.

As you know, the special charity I'm supporting with The Game is the eradication of adult illiteracy. What if companies all across America encouraged employees, using The Game's technology, to volunteer time at literacy organizations in every major city? What if companies sponsored charity fundraisers to benefit these literacy organizations? What if we all decided that adult illiteracy, with its debilitating consequences to individuals and society, must receive our time, money, and attention?

A special rule for The Work Game is:
Lead your business, company, organization,
or neighborhood into playing The Game and
having a group higher purpose.

Work Game Exercises

Do the following exercises if you decide to make The Work Game one of the three to five aspects of life you want to improve in 90 days. Also, design The Work Game by using The Game's basic elements described in Part III of this book: goals, To-Be and Not-To-Be lists, points, prizes, rules, Before-and-After Display, essays, skills, rewards, consequences, deadlines, partners, and coaches.

Exercise: What I Don't Like about Work

For this exercise, you probably won't have to give much thought to the aspects of your work that you dislike most. For The Work Game, you're going to give yourself points as you learn to love these elements of work by becoming present to them through attentiveness. One way to cultivate becoming more productive and appreciative of your work is to start your day by getting your most difficult and important tasks done first. This will eliminate a lot of avoidance behaviors.

Set aside focus time for a task that you really don't like about your job. Use the techniques you've learned in this book to make yourself fully present to the task by putting your attention on it. Then really study that aspect of your work and become a master of it.

EXERCISE: MY FEARS OF FAILURE

Devise a list of all the things you avoid concerning your current work, or a career you want to have in the future. These should be the tasks or aspects of the work that you fear most. Share this list with your Game-partner, and have a "No Fear" day or a "Scaredy Cats" day. Then dive in and go for whatever you fear the most on that one day. Even if you only take the tiniest step toward facing your fear, give yourself points for doing so, and let your partner coach and encourage you.

Break down the things you fear into bite-size pieces. Then focus on the individual steps, rather than on the larger, all-encompassing goal.

EXERCISE: YOUR NATURAL GIFTS AND TALENTS

Pretend you're a news reporter interviewing people about you. Let them know about The Game you're playing and what you hope to discover about yourself and your life. Report back to people you interview and tell them what you've learned from their comments. Be sure to ask others what kind of job or career they could see you doing. Think about putting information from these interviews into your To-Be lists and making them into goals for the next 90 days.

Exercise: Transforming Your Work Environment

Ask people in your office what they'd like to change about your work environment. What would improve their productivity and make them feel inspired? Then talk with your supervisors and see if you can help create changes in the work environment based on the employees' comments.

Also, think about what you would like your boss to do for you to make your work environment better, and then do exactly that for him or her. You may be surprised to find that what you give . . . is also what you get.

If you're adopting a special program or system for The Work Game, give yourself points for using it. An example of a consequence for not achieving goals in The Work Game would be to hold a concert for the entire staff featuring you singing, "That's the sound of the man working on the chain gang." You could also take on a consequence such as becoming the office fax or copier-jam repairperson. Refer to **TheGameInteractive.com** Website for more ideas and coaching specifically targeted to improving your performance in The Work Game.

Use the information in Part I of this book in the chapters "Time," "Structure," "Affinity," "Community," and "Purpose" to balance and coordinate The Work Game with your overall Game plan.

✳ ✳ ✳

In the next chapter, you're going to discover how to fulfill your own higher purpose by serving people and organizations that help others.

✳ ✳ ✳

★ Chapter 17 ★

Your Charities

Duncan Campbell used $2 million from the sale of his investment firm to found a nonprofit organization, Friends of Children, which operates out of an old, rundown building in the Portland, Oregon, neighborhood where he grew up. Duncan hires mentors at beginning teachers' salaries who take the time to help out troubled first-graders until they graduate from high school. Duncan Campbell is giving these children a chance for a better future.

Harvard-educated Dan Pallotta founded Pallotta TeamWorks in 1992. Today, Dan's firm is headquartered in Los Angeles, with approximately 240 full-time employees in 17 offices around the nation. The company has raised $250 million through charitable events, with more than 58 percent of the money going directly toward their causes. Pallotta TeamWorks organizes four "AIDS Rides" across the nation and nine "Breast Cancer 3-Day" walks, which, to date, have drawn more than 50,000 people and inspired millions of Americans to donate. Dan's company has raised more money more quickly for AIDS and breast cancer than any private event operation in U.S. history.

If Duncan and Dan can make a difference in the world, do they hold up the torch for all of us?

I think they do. And this is why I'd like you to consider playing The Charities Game for an aspect of your life you'd most like to improve in 90 days.

Charities Come Later

Perhaps you feel, as many people do, that it takes all your time and energy to live from day to day and raise your family. When you receive requests for donations, flip to a telethon on television, or find that a friend is running in a charity marathon, you probably feel a twinge of guilt that you're not doing more. Now, for 90 days, you can help the charities you've wanted to contribute to by organizing The Charities Game.

First, refer back to your statement of higher purpose and the goals you've been formulating as part of your Game. Next, decide if there is a church or charity that aligns with your higher purpose and goals. Then, enlist as large a community as you can to play The Game and raise money for this charity or charities.

Of course, you'll need to run these ideas for organizing a Charities Game by those in charge of the charity or cause. Get their support and help in figuring out the logistics for contacting regular contributors and members of their organization. Then you'll talk to your friends, neighbors, and co-workers to tell them about this book, your higher purpose, and what you want to do for the charity. Then you'll ask for pledges, donations, and volunteers to play The Charities Game. The Charities Game-players would get as many pledges as possible from people who promise to make donations when the Game-player completes his or her 90-day Charities Game.

Each person who plays The Game can raise money for the charities you've chosen, or their own favorite causes. The race each player will run for The Charities Game isn't a physical one. Instead, each volunteer will play The Game for 90 days using The Game's technology and registering for The Game contest prizes. The more people who play The Game, the more money you'll raise for charity, and the more human beings will win their lives in 90 days. The Charities Game automatically creates structure, affinity, and community, as groups of people gather to share what their higher purposes are and offer suggestions and support for one another's Games. Volunteers can select each other as partners and coaches for their Games. If the Game-players want to do so, they can set group goals that further the higher purpose of the charity as well as their personal goals.

In addition to all the win-win benefits of playing The Charities Game, the cause you're supporting won't have the burden of paying for marketing or facility rental costs to raise this money, so pledged donations will go directly toward benefiting the goals of the organization instead of paying for overhead. The Charities Game can offer a steady supply of income, because volunteers can play their Games for any 90 days, collect pledges, and donate them to the charities year-round.

A special rule for The Charities Game is:
Organize volunteers to collect pledged donations for their completion of The Game.

Making The Charities Game Mean More to You

You're going to have a great time playing The Charities Game just by virtue of all you accomplish and the wonderful volunteers you meet. But I suggest that you also focus on your own level of volunteerism and use The Game's technology to develop whatever else is important in your life.

For example, you could set goals and give yourself points every time you volunteer your time for any charity or church. You could gain points for making new friends among the other volunteers or people whom the charity serves. Each time people ask for your help, whether it's related to the charity or not, you can award points to yourself for responding to their requests. As you acquire positive behaviors and new social and public speaking skills by volunteering and organizing The Charities Game, give yourself rewards.

You're soon to find, though, that charity really is its own reward. At least, that's what Game-player Mary Wichmann discovered.

Mary says:

> As part of my Game, I decided to become a hospice volunteer in my community. After going through the training and orientation, I was given my first assignment with a man named Phil. My goal was to give his wife an hour of free time from her caregiving duties. So while Phil's wife took a break, I held his hand and listened to him talk. As our time together came to an end, Phil didn't want to let go of my hand. It seemed to mean so much for him to have someone who cared enough to just be there and listen.
>
> I found out later that 12 hours after I'd given my love and attention to Phil, he died. I can't tell you how honored I felt to have been with him during his last hours on this earth. I only hope I was able to make some small difference in his life.

A special rule for The Charities Game is:
Design goals and points to support your
own growth as a charity volunteer.

How I Can Help You

When you register to play The Game, let us know on the official registration form if you're playing The Charities Game.

At the end of 90 days, if you've had 10 percent of the regular donors or members of the charitable organization play The Charities Game, you can write to: TCE Associates, 402 West Broadway, Suite 400, San Diego, CA 92101 to request that a certified Game-Master speak to your entire organization. By doing so, the organization can raise more pledges and have more volunteers playing The Game. We'll ask for testimonials from you and others who have already played The Game for 90 days to tell the rest of the organization and their staff what benefits you've derived and how you've won your lives.

As you know from previous chapters, I'm especially concerned with supporting charities that deal with eradicating adult illiteracy. So if you've chosen to play The Charities Game for an adult literacy organization in your community, you'll receive preferential treatment when it comes to getting a Game-Master to speak to your particular organization.

As The Game evolves, I'll be posting more information on **TheGameInteractive.com** Website about special events and donations that **TheCoachingProgram.com** and I will be supporting and hosting to benefit adult literacy organizations nationwide, so check the Website to see what events and activities you might volunteer for in your area.

A special rule for The Charities Game is:
***If 10 percent of the members or donors have
completed the first Charities Game you've organized,
request that a Game-Master speak to the group.***

My Life Is Fine

Sometimes after I've given a motivational speech about our coaching program to a large group of people, someone will come up to me and say, "My life is fine. Why should I put all this effort into playing The Game? Why do I need this now? Why should my work benefit people outside of my family, personal friends, and business associates?"

I explain that while they're focused on themselves, I'm concentrating on the world they'll leave behind for their children and mine. Success isn't only for their benefit, but for the good of all life. Why would they want to make a lot of money and be alone, with no one else to share it with? True success is shared throughout the community. At the same time, we're in no position to help anyone until we've helped ourselves. So playing The Charities Game accomplishes both purposes. I ask, "What are you willing to have happen in your personal universe that would put you into a powerful position for sharing with the world at large?"

Some respond by letting these words sink deeply into their hearts and become the most mature players of The Game. Others shake their heads and walk away, smugly content with their lives, or unwilling to accept my challenge to display what magnificent human beings they could be.

Which type of person are you?

EXERCISES FOR THE CHARITIES GAME

Use the activities described with the special rules above if you decide to make The Charities Game one of the three to five aspects of life you want to improve in 90 days. Also, design The Charities Game by using The Game's basic elements described in Part III of this book: goals, To-Be and Not-To-Be lists, points, prizes, rules, Before-and-After Displays, essays, skills, rewards, consequences, deadlines, partners, and coaches.

If you're adopting a special program or system for The Charities Game, give yourself points for using it. An example of a consequence for not achieving goals in The Charities Game would be to offer to mop all the floors or clean all the bathrooms at the charity's headquarters if you fail to make a difference or if you stop your efforts before 90 days. Refer to **TheGameInteractive.com** Website for more ideas and coaching specifically targeted to improving your performance in The Charities Game.

Use the information in Part I of this book in the chapters "Time," "Structure," "Affinity," "Community," and "Purpose" to balance and coordinate The Charities Game with your overall Game plan.

✳ ✳ ✳

You're almost to the finish line when it comes to reading about the many choices you can focus on for 90 days. In the next chapter, you'll learn about a Game that will make you think I've saved the best for last.

✳ ✳ ✳

★ CHAPTER 18 ★

Your Hobbies, Interests, and Art

Please don't think that because this is the *last* section in those that discuss different aspects of life . . . that it's the least. Playing The Hobbies, Interests, and Art (HIA) Game may prove to be the most enlightening, entertaining, and amazing way to expand your horizons in only 90 days.

Out of all the aspects of life, hobbies, interests, and art may be what you most put off for "someday" and "later." This could be making you lose balance by overusing your mind, body, and spirit in some ways, and woefully underusing and under-developing yourself in others. Pursuing and becoming proficient at creative endeavors allows you to develop a whole new set of skills, and puts you in touch with entirely new communi-ties and structures. You're also likely to use different parts of your body and brain when you develop a hobby, sport, or inter-est outside of your work arena.

You may have always considered pleasurable pursuits to be irrelevant. But taking up the practice of a sport or art could be the very thing that turns you from being an idiot savant into a Renaissance man or woman. Instead of only being accom-plished in one or two areas of life, you'll develop several activ-ities with some proficiency while you play The HIA Game. This allows you to win your life in entirely new ways.

Many people who think they're dissatisfied with their work aren't really that unhappy with it at all. But by only working and not having any hobbies, interests, or art, they're stifling their creative energy. They're neglecting needs that work or a job can't be expected to fulfill.

As his hobby, one of **TheCoachingProgram.com** clients transformed a rugged, uncared-for piece of land into a beautiful and expansive garden when he played The HIA Game. He says that sitting in this garden is now where he finds the most peace and tranquility.

Finding the Time to Play

I had the opportunity to work on model boat building with my ex-father-in-law when he was in his early 60s. I was amazed to see that due to a lifetime of practicing this hobby, he was able to thread a needle significantly better than I could. As he was growing older, instead of becoming more feeble, his physical coordination skills were actually expanding. Plus, he was enjoying a hobby that kept him interested in his life.

Maybe you're someone who has told yourself that you can't make time in your busy life to have hobbies, play a sport, or pursue an interest in art. For 90 days during The HIA Game, you'll take that time for yourself to do *A Activities* with an *A Relationship*—namely you. You'll also have the opportunity to develop new *A Relationships* with others who are interested in the same things you are. As you reprioritize to balance and expand your life, your self-esteem will also improve.

Let's say you're someone who says, "I love to read, but I never have the time," or "I really like movies, but I rarely go to them," or "I'd love to know more about Civil War history, but I haven't had the opportunity to gain any knowledge of this era." Now, you can once again take a look at your higher purpose and decide which of the thousands of hobbies, interests, and art activities in the world will further the meaning of your life for 90 days. Put these things on your To-Be list for The HIA Game, and see yourself blossom in exhilarating ways.

A special rule for The HIA Game is:
Schedule time every day for a hobby, interest, or art activity that aligns with your higher purpose.

The Value of Practice

Dr. Martin Kettelhut, whom you've met in previous chapters, says that through the study of Jujitsu, which he cultivated while playing The Game, he became more ambidextrous, because this martial art requires functioning equally well with both hands. Before playing The Game, Doc had taken Jujitsu lessons but had rarely found the time to practice. For 90 days, he practiced both mentally and physically.

After a while, he noticed that the practice of putting any instrument in the hand he doesn't use predominately helped him develop finger dexterity. Since he's a classical pianist, this was a very good thing. Later, Dr. Kettelhut read that a person could increase his I.Q. by gaining access to the use of his non-dominant hand. This was an age-old secret embedded long ago in the art of Jujitsu. Playing The Game helped Doc move from just taking classes to practicing and perfecting the skills for a martial art.

One of **TheCoachingProgram.com** clients used The HIA Game to greatly improve his golf game. He began to give golf a level of focus and attention that kept him present for each movement. He noticed his state of mind before swinging at or hitting the ball and realized that whatever he was thinking about affected his stroke.

My client decided to use the skill I've introduced previously in this book and Refresh before swinging at the ball. By doing so, he connected to the game and the moment in a way he never had before. The entire experience went more smoothly, and his skills and golf scores improved. He'd gained access to being "in the zone" at will. Many people only stumble into this kind of presence and focus occasionally, but playing The Game helped this golfer experience it whenever he wished.

A special rule of The HIA Game is:
Mentally and physically practice skills
related to hobbies, interests, and art.

Take It to a Higher Level

When you play The HIA Game and decide which activities you want to turn into goals, you can give yourself points for bringing them to a higher level of efficiency or creating new systems within them. For example, if you want to write, you might develop your craft by reading works by your favorite authors and imitating their styles—perhaps in the style of Ernest Hemingway or Joyce Carol Oates. It makes the writing fun and instructive until you find your own voice.

The development of style or craft within a hobby, art activity, or interest isn't the same as turning it into yet another way to work all the time. The joy of playing The Game is learning balance in all things. Give yourself points for not becoming obsessed with whatever you choose for The HIA Game and keeping it fun, intriguing, and light, if you don't typically tackle new skills and habits this way.

Loy Gotham found that reorganizing and revamping part of her yard allowed her to convert what she called "lumpy, bumpy, rocky, weedy areas" into more than an exercise in creativity.

Loy says:

A section of my yard is too uneven to mow, and it costs a fortune to have the weeds whacked there every week. I already have four large flower, vegetable, and herb gardens; as well as a pond area, woodland path, and a garden glade. I wanted a low-maintenance solution for this wild section of my property.

Some of the rocks in this area weigh more than two tons each and can't be easily moved. I decided I'd try to incorporate a Zen garden into this difficult section of my property. I asked a friend who owns a backhoe and my significant other to help me move whatever rocks we could, and try to level out this area as much as possible. I bought some books on Zen gardening. I discovered that one of the "rules" for creating such a garden is that the horizontal rocks should be 10 to 30 percent of the size of the vertical rocks. I couldn't get these proportions to work at all. In that past, this kind of imperfection would have driven me nuts. But The Game was helping me learn how to just go with the flow, which is, after all, the Zen philosophy.

I had to accept that mine wouldn't be a traditional Japanese Zen garden, but it could reflect the Zen of the Minnesota Iron Range where I live by having a bench and fountain. Building this garden during my 90-day Game gave me access to a new level of flexibility. I was able to creatively visualize an "Iron Range" Zen garden and have fun with that theme. It felt wonderful to let go of my need to make everything perfect and to enjoy my garden for its natural beauty and as a lovely, peaceful haven.

A special rule of the HIA Game is:
Don't turn what you do for pleasure
into work or self-criticism.

The graceful development of a hobby, art activity, or interest can become one of the greatest gifts you've ever given yourself. You'll reap such unexpected benefits that you'll wonder why you've waited so long to treat yourself to more of the pleasurable things life has to offer.

EXERCISES FOR YOUR HOBBIES, INTERESTS, AND ART ACTIVITIES

Use the activities described with the special rules above if you decide to make The HIA Game one of the three to five aspects of life you want to improve in 90 days. Also, design The HIA Game by using The Game's basic elements described in Part III of this book: goals, To-Be and Not-To-Be lists, points, prizes, rules, Before-and-After Displays, essays, skills, rewards, consequences, deadlines, partners, and coaches.

If you're adopting a special program or system for The HIA Game, give yourself points for using it. An example of a consequence for not achieving goals in The HIA Game would be that you'll have to walk around home and work with a sign on your back that says, "I'm a one-dimensional person." Refer to **TheGameInteractive.com** Website for more ideas and coaching specifically targeted to improving your performance in The HIA Game.

Use the information in Part I of this book in the chapters "Time," "Structure," "Affinity," "Community," and "Purpose" to balance and coordinate The HIA Game with your overall Game plan.

✻ ✻ ✻

Now that you've read about the possible aspects of life you could improve by playing The Game, it's time to start making some decisions. In the last section of this book, you'll be designing your personalized Game Playing Field.

✳ ✳ ✳

⋆ PART III ⋆

How to Play The Game

*"The real lesson is that there is no limit to what
we can do. It's incredibly empowering to watch
yourself move slowly but unmistakably toward a
goal. You have to break down your dream into
simple steps and then DO them. For a while, you
make lists and count points and brag about your
accomplishments. Then a strange thing happens—at least it happened to me. I got tired of
counting. I forgot my list. I broke all the rules.
AND THE GAME STILL WORKED!*

*"Then, when I had to write an essay at the end
of 90 days, I discovered that I'd done everything,
even more than I set out to do. I seem to have
emerged from playing The Game with the sense
that I can do anything, if I have the patience and
persistence to try. I have undeniable, three-dimen-
sional evidence that whatever goal I'm pointed at
is entirely within my reach. I just need to have
faith and keep taking one step at a time."*

— **Bess Turner, Player of The Game**

⋆ CHAPTER 19 ⋆

The Game Playing Field

Now it's time to design your personalized Game Playing Field. You're probably brimming with ideas about which aspects of life you most want to improve. You'll be selecting three to five of them for playing your first 90-day Game. Remember, you can always play again to continue adding new levels of accomplishments.

Here's the sequence for filling in "The Playing Field for Your Game." First, at the top of The Playing Field for Your Game, write your statement of purpose, as you understand it so far. Ask yourself in which aspects of life you're most or least aligned with your higher purpose.

Next, rate yourself on how effective you are in each of the major aspects of life that you have read about in Part II of this book.

Refer to the filled-in model of The Game Playing Field on the next page as an example, and copy the blank Game Playing Field from page 227 to complete your personal Game Playing Field.

You'll shade in the box in the number-one rating column if you believe you have little or no mastery of that area. You'll shade in all ten boxes for an area you think you've completely mastered. For each area of life, fill in the boxes from one to ten, rating yourself on how effective you consider yourself to be in them.

The Playing Field for Your Game

Your Higher Purpose

Aspects of Your Life	Rating 1 2 3 4 5 6 7 8 9 10	Your Goals
Body & Health	▓▓▓	*Get to ideal weight.*
Money	▓▓▓▓▓	
Relationships	▓▓▓▓▓	
Spiritual Life	▓	*Learn the purpose of my life.*
Mind	▓▓▓	*Have sharper focus & attention on everything I do and say.*
Tools	▓▓▓▓▓▓▓	
Community	▓▓▓▓	
Environment	▓▓▓▓	
Education	▓▓▓▓▓▓	
Family	▓▓▓▓▓▓	
Work	▓▓▓▓▓▓▓	
Charities	▓▓	*Volunteer to teach someone to read.*
Hobbies/ Interests/Art	▓▓▓	*Have an art gallery display of my nature photography.*

The Playing Field for Your Game

Your Higher Purpose											
Aspects of Your Life	**Rating** 1 2 3 4 5 6 7 8 9 10										**Your Goals**
Body & Health											
Money											
Relationships											
Spiritual Life											
Mind											
Tools											
Community											
Environment											
Education											
Family											
Work											
Charities											
Hobbies/ Interests/Art											

How to Choose Areas for Your Playing Field

After you've finished filling in the ratings on your Playing Field, you'll choose three to five areas of life to focus on while playing your Game. Game-player Loy Gotham offers some good advice on choosing areas for improvements. She says, "Don't be too hard on yourself. Choose a few things that are really important to you for your first Game. You can always play again to work on other areas."

By analyzing The Playing Field for Your Game, it will immediately be visually clear where your life needs improvement by how many boxes you've filled in for each area. You probably have a pretty good idea by now where you have work to do, but at this point, you can also consult your community by asking others to rate your effectiveness in the areas of The Game's Playing Field.

Before you make your final decision about which areas to focus on for your Game, this is a good time to really reflect on your statement of purpose. Think about those aspects of life that would further the higher purpose of your life during the next 90 days. Consider this information as you make your final decisions on what to focus on.

Also, look at what you wrote for the exercises "Dying Without Regret" and "My Eulogy." The areas where you feel you've had the most accomplishments and touched people most deeply will be the most satisfying. Choose the least satisfying areas, which contain guilt and regret, for your Game Playing Field so you can expand your muscles and grow in them.

Take into consideration the information you attained by doing the exercise, "What Are You Really Up To?" Your ineffective roles can point to areas of improvement for your Game. Compare the percentages you gave yourself for effectiveness in the various roles you play with how you've rated yourself in the aspects of life. For example, did you rate yourself as an ineffective parent? Would that low rating make you consider playing The Family Game?

Before you make your final selection of the three to five areas for your Game, let's recap criteria you need to use:

- Which areas do you have to improve upon to fulfill your higher purpose?

- Which areas are you least content with—the ones that contain the most guilt and regret?

- In which roles have you rated yourself as most ineffective?

- Which areas contain aspects that you've always wanted to develop but have never found the time or resources to pursue?

- As you analyze this data, where do you think your life is out of balance?

The categories represented in your Game are aspects of life where you're not entirely complete or satisfied with yourself. Your Game, like your life, is entirely subjective. At the end of The Game and your life, you'll get to say whether or not it was happy or successful.

After you've selected the areas you'll focus on for The Game, record them in your Game journal and post them places that will remind yourself and others what these next 90 days will be all about for you. Remember to gain the support of your communities for the magnificent decision to win your life in 90 days.

✶ ✶ ✶

CHAPTER 20

Goals

When you play any game, one of your goals is to win. You'll probably have other goals, too—to have fun, to socialize, and to test and build your strength and endurance.

Playing The Game, as you've seen in the previous chapters, means that you'll set goals that you want to achieve in 90 days. But The Game's goals are different from others you've had in your life so far. To play The Game full out, you'll want your goals to be beyond your reach, unrealistic, crazy, stupid, unbelievable, and absolutely amazing. That's when your goals will motivate you. These are the kind of goals that compel instead of compromise.

The planet belongs to people who have big goals. Don't let your goal-setting be limited by what you can figure out right now. How to fulfill your goals will become more clear as you refine, plan for, and visualize yourself doing them. Get ready to reap all the benefits of going for "unrealistic" goals. Dr. Kettelhut says, "Climbing Mount Kilimanjaro was my most self-fulfilling experience. I really had to put myself aside to accomplish every task at hand. I've never felt so peaceful and deeply satisfied in my life as I did on the plane ride home from Africa."

Allow me to scramble your brains even further with the

next thought: *It makes absolutely no difference at all whether you're successful at achieving your goals. All that matters is playing The Game for 90 days. Your goals will take care of themselves.*

Better Goals Make for Better Obstacles

It's inevitable that setting goals produces obstacles. No goals means no obstacles—the life of your typical couch potato. Bigger goals produce bigger obstacles—the life of a hero. Obstacles are a natural outcome of shaking and rattling your life. While playing The Game, I'm suggesting that you sit down at least once each day and express gratitude for the stumbling blocks in your way, for these are your stepping-stones to greatness.

In The Game, instead of letting obstacles stop you, allow your imagination and the power of structure, affinity, and community to help you discover ingenious ways of getting things done. When you start overlooking, dodging, breaking through, or handling obstacles, you're likely to realize another very important truth about them: Obstacles are imaginary; they're puffs of smoke.

You carefully construct your own obstacles, telling yourself they're insurmountable, and then you delay dealing with them in the hopes that they'll go away. Then you complain about them.

How has that game been working for you?

Would you like to try a different Game?

After you've set your goals for The Game, go back to your Game journal and write down *all* the obstacles you think you might meet. Be sure to make them big and scary—you'll lose your job, you'll go bankrupt, your spouse will leave you, and your kids will pierce many of their body parts and call from another state to tell you about it. Think of the worst things that could possibly happen if you were to play wholeheartedly to achieve your goals. Now ask yourself, "Could I survive this?" If the answer is yes, no matter how "unrealistic" the goal is, keep it in your Game.

While you play The Game, analyze your setbacks for the valuable information they contain. This is what I mean by taking life as coaching. Discover how you've constructed your failures so you can deconstruct them. Even a bad plan, if executed, will teach you something. If you make mistakes, it means you can be coached.

Breaking Down Obstacles

Break down immense goals into pieces you can achieve right now. Tiny goals equal tiny obstacles. Ninety days of doing anything to overcome your obstacles and achieve your goals will get you moving in some positive direction.

I've met people, including myself, who say they don't have time to write. I ask, "Could you write one sentence every day?" Of course they can handle this. My next question is, "If you wrote a sentence each day, since the first time you thought about writing a book, how much of that book would be written by now?" The answer is usually, "All of it."

The Value of Persistence

If you take a deeper look at your life, you'll see that all of your successes were preceded by, or are the result of, your failures. Success and failure are a circular life motion. Who's to say where this circle begins or ends? And why would you label one part of the circle negative and the other part positive? Your last incredible failures may be bringing access to your next major successes. If you're busy judging every movement with the "success" or "failure" labels, you freeze yourself into inaction.

While playing The Game, it's imperative that you follow a basic rule: *At the end of each day, reframe anything you've tended to view as failure, and accept that it could be a step toward success.* Every day during the next 90 days offers the opportunity for a fresh start. Every moment is a chance to begin with renewed vigor.

When you fall, and you will if you're really playing, get back up. When you fall again, get up. Stop thinking and get into motion. This is persistence. This is The Game.

If your higher purpose is worth fulfilling, it's worth failing at. If you're someone who has always calculated the possibility of success before setting any goals, then now is the time to end that kind of limited thinking and planning. The Game will go to the most earnest individual. This is the person who persists in the face of challenges.

Think of times in your life when you tried and stopped. What would have happened if you'd stayed the course? How many attempts do you usually make before you give up on a goal? Estimate this number and put it on your Before-and-After Display. Amaze yourself with what happens in 90 days of not stopping each time you fall.

Play The Game as if you're serious about your goals. Let everybody, including you, know that this time you're not settling for less. But allow yourself to be happy no matter what happens, because the greatest winner of all is the one who has played.

To-Be and Not-To-Be Lists

To play The Game, you'll be focusing on three to five aspects of life that you most want to improve. You'll put the goals that you want to initiate or have more of in your life on what I call a "To-Be" list. This is different from a "To-Do" list, which is a compilation of the ways you intend to spend your time and the things you intend to do.

With the To-Be list, you'll know exactly who and what you want to be in life. The goals on this list should be broad, expansive, and inspiring.

Below are examples for To-Be lists that you can use as models.

To-Be:
- More flexible
- Physically stronger
- More persistent
- More devoted to family
- Adept at using new technology
- More tolerant

The other type of list you'll create for each aspect of life you want to improve in 90 days is a "Not-To-Be" list. This is a way of thinking about goals for what you want to eliminate or decrease in your life.

The following are examples of goals you might put on your Not-To-Be list.

Not-To-Be:
- Late
- Crabby
- Inconsiderate
- Wasteful
- Daydreaming or absentminded
- Blaming others for my problems

As you construct these lists, remember not to be concerned about how you'll achieve these goals.

In the next chapter, we'll talk about breaking down your To-Be and Not-To-Be lists into smaller tasks, behaviors, and habits and giving yourself points to help you accomplish goals with the technology of The Game.

✳ ✳ ✳

CHAPTER 21

Points and Scores

The point of The Game . . . is to figure out the point of The Game. To do this, you have to give yourself points.

Huh?

Now that you've developed your To-Be and Not-To-Be lists, it's time to break down your goals into discreet tasks and behaviors for achieving them. The process of scoring and giving yourself points acknowledges every time you stretch yourself. At the end of The Game, the points you've accumulated will be irrelevant, because what matters is who you've become, not how many points you've scored.

Points for Whatever Is Hard to Do

Before playing The Game, you'll make a list of the habits you want to develop or eliminate. You'll decide exactly what tasks will help you achieve your goals, and establish new behaviors. During The Game, you'll use this list and give yourself one point each time you do something difficult or perform an action you don't usually do. These are what I call *conscious acts of will.* For example, if one of your goals on your To-Be List is to have excellent dental hygiene but you always forget to floss, you'd give yourself one point for each time you floss.

If flossing becomes a habit before your 90-day Game is over, or you start to find great pleasure in doing it, you should stop giving yourself points for running that little thread through the cracks between your teeth. Instead, you might get a point each time you massage your gums if you're not already doing that.

Give yourself points for tasks and habits that will eliminate behaviors and patterns you no longer want in your life. For example, if you wanted to be less self-righteous, you can give yourself a point each time you admit you could be wrong. If a goal on your Not-To-Be list is to eliminate or decrease alcohol consumption, you could award a point every time someone offers you a drink and you turn it down.

Increase your motivation by awarding points to yourself for tiny increments of a task you don't want to do. For example, if you dislike washing dishes but you don't want to leave them in the sink anymore, give yourself a point for getting up and washing at least one dish.

My daughter, Georgia, gives herself a point every time she cleans up after herself, does her homework without complaining, and studies for math tests. Here are a few more suggestions to help you design your point system.

You can give yourself a point each time you:

- remember someone's name,
- do sit-ups,
- hug your child,
- eat fiber,
- learn a new function of your computer,
- pray or meditate, and
- listen without interrupting.

Be sure to take opportunities for awarding points when you multitask and accomplish one or more nonconflicting tasks at once. For example, what if you read spiritual literature or scripture while walking on a treadmill (two points)? If you wanted to spend more time with your child, could you coach a team he's on, always be on time for practices, and refrain from criticizing him (three points)? Find many ways to increase your scores, and challenge yourself by using points as an incentive.

Taking Away Points

Look over your Not-To-Be list of goals, which show the behaviors, attitudes, and habits you intend to eliminate in 90 days. Also, review the basic rules of The Game. When you do things that don't support your Not-To-Be list or break one of the basic rules of The Game, take away points. When you catch yourself and reverse the unwanted action, give yourself a point.

For example, a basic rule of The Game is that you won't criticize yourself for 90 days. When you tally points, remember those moments when you indulged in self-criticism. Deduct points for those slip-ups. By deducting points, especially at the start of the 90-day period, you may drop below zero points into the negative numbers. But guess what? This is a good thing. It shows that you're starting to develop self-awareness and are becoming conscious.

Give yourself a point when you have a critical thought about yourself, catch it immediately, and reverse this thought by replacing it with a positive affirmation about yourself. This is how you use points to become aware of and eliminate unwanted behavior and habits.

Analyzing Your Points

Keeping score with The Game will help you recognize what you're not really committed to, or things you intended to do that aren't working toward fulfilling your purpose. When you notice that you're not making points for certain behaviors or tasks, ask yourself if they're important to you or redundant. If you admit that it's not a matter of giving up, but you're just never going to institute this habit, then take it off your list without feeling any guilt.

You can drop items and goals with ease when you see that they don't fulfill your purpose after all. Then you'll have more time and energy to focus your attention on what you *do* want out of your life. In this way, The Game is very much about self-regulation. You're developing an internal gyroscope to guide you toward true north, your higher purpose.

Keeping Score and Tallying Points

You can use any device that is convenient for keeping score. This can be as simple as carrying a small notebook or clicking a counter to tally points. Write the number of points in your Game journal each day, and compare your progress from the beginning to the end of The Game.

Later, I'll be going into more detail about your Game's partner and coaches. It's fun to compete with your partner for The Game to see who can score the most number of points for a day, week, or month. You can give each other prizes and consequences for scoring points.

You can't really cheat at The Game, because this isn't the kind of homework you could do the night before a test. In 90 days, the points mean nothing. The only thing that counts is what has happened in your life. In what areas, and how much, have you improved? There's no faking those things.

I've seen people earn up to 100 points in a day. Some are scoring 1,000 points per day by the end of their three-month Game.

Have fun with points and scoring. You're making all of this up as you go along. It's *your* Game. Just remember to acknowledge yourself as you do what you said you'd do, and forget about false humility. It's time to shout from the rooftops about the life you're winning.

✶ ✶ ✶

★ Chapter 22 ★

Prizes

The single biggest prize in The Game is your life. The Game's results show up in the life you win as you become profoundly present to the majesty of your own existence. Playing The Game will restore and heighten your gratitude for life.

The tangible proof of what you can do and be as a human being in the form of your Before-and-After Displays, your essay, and the profound difference you've made in other people's lives are prizes you'll always treasure and can pass along to your children and grandchildren. You'll be able to show them what is possible for a human being to become in 90 days of concentrated attention and focus.

An additional prize that playing The Game offers is the companionship and support of community. You'll begin to hear the roar of the fans cheering you on. With community, you'll gain the resources and encouragement to accomplish anything. Your communities can be a lifelong source of comfort, joy, and friendship.

Another prize you'll reap from The Game is the coaching from your Game partner. When you begin playing The Game, it might be hard to imagine that this person you've chosen to be your confidante and coach will become a welcomed and valued addition to your life. A partner may get on your nerves, disappoint you, and even irritate you. Your partner will teach you the most about every relationship in your life. You and your Game partner will live in the trenches together. The memories of laughter and tears you share while playing The Game is something neither of you will ever forget.

Don't Wait for Prizes

Don't wait to see if you win prizes by the end of The Game. Reward yourself creatively and often throughout the 90 days. In The Game, you're going to cut through delay tactics and get present to everyday accomplishments.

Instead of being your own worst coach and rarely praising yourself, reward yourself in increments. Follow the business principle of paying yourself first. Think of really juicy ways to reward yourself for completing The Game, but also enjoy the pleasure of acknowledging your accomplishments and attempts.

When you play The Game, get creative about what to use as a reward, depending on which areas of your life you've chosen to improve. For example, if you're dieting, give yourself a non-food reward by going with a friend to a movie, an evening of entertainment, or a walk in nature. If you work a lot, reward yourself by spending a relaxing evening at home with flowers, candles, and your favorite music. Think of things you enjoy doing but rarely allow yourself the time to indulge in, and turn them into prizes for your Game.

Decide how many points you want to score and by what date; and schedule a weekend, a day, or even an hour with someone special as your reward. Give yourself a 30-day Game party; share your goals, accomplishments, and statement of higher purpose with your guests.

The Prize of Money

The final grand prize for The Game is the money I'm offering to the partners whose essays and personal accomplishments inspire the registered Game-players. As you already know, the grand cash prize for The Game is $50,000.

As I've mentioned previously, the grand prizes include participation in **TheCoachingProgram.com's** 15-month coaching program for the top winners, and four other runner-up teams of partners. This is the equivalent of an $18,000-per-person prize. It offers the opportunity for Game-players to become incredible leaders as they interact with some of the finest people on the planet.

Your Own Prize Money

You and your partner can cook up all kinds of fun and stimulating ways of rewarding yourselves and each other. Don't overlook the possibility of putting up your own prize money for whichever one of you scores the most points and achieves the most goals in 90 days. You can even involve your communities in creating grand-prize money that you can accept for yourself or donate to your favorite charities.

Don't hesitate to use prizes and prize money to keep yourself motivated. Prizes inspire you to put more at stake. This uses a fundamental principle of human nature—people play harder and have more fun when they play to win and the prize is something they really want. It's so simple. It's The Game.

★ ★ ★

★ CHAPTER 23 ★

Rules and Umpires

The Game is an exercise in building determination, deepening attention, and raising your consciousness to the beauty in everyday existence. Like any other game you might play, it uses certain simple rules to guide players through its structure. Playing by the same rules enables everyone to enjoy the fairness, competition, and fun of The Game. There are general rules for The Game, listed below. Use these rules to design your personalized Game.

One of the dichotomies of life is that the people we read about in history books are those who have broken the rules of their respective societies. They went beyond the limitations of the day. They believed that humans could fly, that the earth moved around the sun, and that the world wasn't flat. Many of these courageous individuals were vilified during their lifetimes and were only honored after death.

Bending Rules

I'm encouraging you to play by the rules of The Game. In the same breath, I'm telling you to bend and even break these rules when you think it's necessary to revise or reconsider what you're doing. It is and always will be *your* Game.

Even though I've listed the suggested rules for The Game, there are really no rules except the ones you've agreed to make and abide by. The mature player will undo his or her own chains by adjusting The Game to maximize results and efficiency. The razor's edge will be how to change the rules without offering up the same tired old excuses you've always given for quitting or delaying your life.

Looking at what's going on in your Game and adjusting it accordingly will prevent you from failing. In fact, the only way you can fail is to stop playing before the 90 days is up. By continuing with the process, you're conducting a grand experiment with respect to how your life operates. You'll try some things, and they'll have the same results you've always had, so you'll stop them. You'll make new choices and get new results, so you'll institute the habits that are now more to your liking. Some things you do in The Game will be easy; other things will be hard. You'll stretch by going for the more difficult goals. The Game's rules are only here to provide you with structure and a road map to discover your own great life.

Our Agreements

It's not a rule of The Game, but I'm asking you to make an agreement—to strike a pact with me. I'm willing to share The Game's technology with you, and in return, I ask that you use the strength and determination you gain by playing The Game to benefit all of life. I'm asking that you honor this agreement with me. As long as you use what you learn for the benefit of all, I'm very confident that The Game will uplift you and inspire you. If you go another way and use The Game's technology to harm yourself or others, I don't know what the consequences will be.

The most important agreement you'll make by registering

to play The Game, of course, is the one you've made with yourself. The Game is about keeping commitments to yourself and others. The agreements you break the most are the ones people will most often break with you. By playing The Game, you'll start eliminating those areas where you're not keeping commitments, and start living up to your principles and values by achieving your goals honorably.

General Rules for The Game

Below are the general operating instructions for The Game. I suggest that you copy these basic rules and post them in places where you'll be reminded of them frequently. Remember, you should give yourself a point each time you keep these rules, and deduct a point when you break them.

- Play The Game for 90 days.
- Observe what you're learning by playing The Game.
- Remember that The Game is a shared journey and a process.
- Don't criticize yourself.
- No whining for 90 days.
- No gossiping.
- Do *A Activities* with *A Relationships* during most of your day.
- Invite everyone to support you, but don't push your Game on anyone.
- At the end of each day, reframe anything you've tended to view as failure, and accept that it could be a step toward success.

- Give yourself points for doing only difficult or nonhabitual acts.

- Reward yourself throughout the 90 days.

- Break big goals into smaller tasks, and give yourself points for accomplishing each increment.

- Keep a weekly Game journal of your challenges and achievements.

- Increase your reading speed, and give yourself points for doing speed-reading exercises.

- Refresh upon waking, before going to sleep, and between activities. Give yourself points for increasing the number of times each day that you Refresh.

- Alternate Refreshing with operating at high velocity.

- Multitask efficiently, with attention.

- Integrate complementary tasks seamlessly.

- Set up funny, embarrassing, but nonharmful consequences you're unwilling to pay, and tell your communities about them.

- Set up monthly or weekly deadlines for achieving your goals.

- Select a partner, and help your partner win The Game. Give points for coaching each other on ten-minute daily calls.

- Keep your coaching information confidential.

- When you can't keep your commitments (especially to your partner and your daily calls together), let your partner know before the appointed time.

- Have fun!

Umpires and Referees

In any game, there's a referee or an umpire who enforces the rules and arbitrates differences among players. In The Game, I'm the referee and umpire because I've made up this technology. However, I'm not with you every day, so you're going to have to become your own umpire. You can't even expect your partner to do this for you. In fact, I've seen some partners get into debates and disputes over how many points they each deserve. This is a ridiculous waste of time and energy. No one but you knows whether you've been operating at your full potential. You're the only person who can decide whether something you've done is worthy of scoring a point.

None of these aspects—rules, points, lists, rewards—matter in the long run. They're only in place to give you a structure and help you have more fun by competing, acknowledging yourself, and keeping track of your progress. In 90 days, you'll reap results that will speak for themselves. The end result of The Game will become your ultimate umpire and referee. Life is your umpire. Winning your life is winning The Game.

In the next chapter, you're going to learn one of the most interesting and wonderful parts of playing The Game. It's how you chart and acknowledge all the progress you've made, and the goals you've accomplished in only 90 days.

✶ ✶ ✶

CHAPTER 24

Before-and-After Displays and Essays

Two of the most rewarding elements of playing The Game are the displays and written documents you'll create to visually and verbally depict your results. These are your Before-and-After Displays and the essays you'll write about your progress. They express and articulate the pronounced changes you've made within areas of your life where you've created a shift and can now show it. Before-and-After Displays and essays communicate to yourself and others that you've spent your time and energy well by playing The Game. With these elements, you'll creatively share your breakthroughs, knowledge, and achievements.

All too often we don't notice or document what's happening in our lives. We attempt to do things and may think we've failed, when in fact, we may have made significant progress. For a Before-and-After Display in one of The Games I played, I kept meticulous records of the points I accumulated each day and what categories they were in. This meant that on my displays I was able to keep track of my commitments. This documentation turned out to be a very powerful reinforcement for me. In the past, I'd always been aware of how often I broke commitments but rarely noticed how many I was keeping. After I recorded points for the hundreds of commitments I kept during my Game, I decreased the number I broke. This is because I was now enjoying playing a Game where I rewarded myself for accomplishments instead of feeling bad about what I didn't do.

You can keep your Before-and-After Displays and essays for the rest of your life to remind you of how special you are. They show that for 90 days you learned that you can and do make a difference. Some people write their memoirs, so these materials documenting your Game may be the beginning of that kind of project for you. You can share Before-and-After Displays and essays with your children and grandchildren to show them what it's possible for a human being to accomplish in a very short time.

Examples of Before-and-After Displays

You can make your display by using large pieces of poster board that can be purchased at any office-supply store. Paste photos and other documents on it with spray mount. Keep your Before Display visible to remind you and others what you're trying to accomplish with The Game and why. Take photos of your Before-and-After Displays, and keep them in a safe place. If you and your partner are chosen as finalists in The Game, we'll ask you to submit these photos. Then we'll post them on **TheGameInteractive.com's** Website, where other registered Game-players can look at them, and read your essays.

Below are some additional examples that may inspire and stimulate ideas for your displays. The idea is to make these visual displays as strong and clear as possible so that when your Game is over you'll have a record of what's possible for you in your life.

Before-and-After Displays can include the following:

- Photos of sections of your yard that you've transformed with gardens and landscaping

- Photos of messy and cluttered closets, drawers, dark attics, and cabinets in disarray that you've organized and cleared out

- A page from your day-planner that shows how you spend time on an average day, contrasted with a page that shows your effectiveness by the end of The Game

- Results of medical tests such as cholesterol, blood pressure, percentage of body fat, measurements, and weight

- Photos of you from different angles in a swimming suit, holding the day's newspaper to verify the dates these photos were taken

- A videotape accompanying your displays showing you talking about your attitudes and view of life before and after playing The Game

- Collages of pictures cut out from magazines depicting your progress with emotional issues you're working on for The Game—such as patience, compassion, or anger

- Photos of people in your communities showing how many more people you're relating to by the end of 90 days

- A copy of your Christmas or holiday card list showing how many more people will be getting cards from you this year

- If you've had breakdowns in communication with friends or family members, photos of you with that person or even hosting a family reunion or dinner

- If there are people you've neglected to keep up with, show copies of e-mails, letters, or long-distance phone bills showing how you've reestablished contact with them
- Your reading speed before and after the 90-day period

Your Essay

Writing an essay is your opportunity to communicate to yourself and the world the profound changes you made, the benefits you and your communities have received from those changes, and how you accomplished your results. Others should be able to read the essays that you and your partner write and gain insight on how to produce the same results.

Writing the essay will be a fun and transformational part of your Game journey. When you send your essay to me to become a contender for The Game's prizes, it not only represents you, but also shows me that you'll be a great spokesperson for The Game. Your essay conveys the impression that you're a leader who can produce fantastic results and communicate them to others.

To help you recall the details that will make your essay come alive, one of the basic rules for The Game is: *Keep a weekly Game journal.* This will reflect the challenges you've faced and accomplishments you've achieved so far. You should include how many points you've won during each week, and any changes in your attitudes and behavior. When you review this journal, it will help you write your essay as a journey from the start to the finish line.

Beyond the 90 days of your Game, you will have acquired skills that can last for a lifetime. In the next chapter, you'll find out what they are and how necessary they'll be to your entire life.

★ Chapter 25 ★

Skills

As with any game, the players need to develop certain skills in order to become proficient and achieve optimum results. The Game is no exception to this rule. You'll acquire special skills to play the Games that deal with aspects of life you want to improve. This chapter will introduce or reiterate the skills you'll need for playing the entire Game.

I've already discussed the skill or habit I call Refresh. This is not only an essential skill to develop for a better spiritual life, it's also crucial to the success of your Game. To Refresh, you'll stop what you're doing, sit comfortably, and breathe in deeply. As you inhale, allow energy, clarity, and peace to enter every fiber of your being. Then exhale; and release all your cares, worries, and agitation.

Refresh when you first wake up in the morning and before you fall asleep at night. Refresh between activities so you don't carry over the success or failure of one project to the next. Use the process of Refreshing as a circuit breaker to allow the past to stay in the past, the present to be the present, and the future to take care of itself.

While playing The Game, constantly alternate Refreshing with moving at high velocity. Think of it as using a spurt of energy to sprint over the finish line and then stopping to rest before going on to the next race. During The Game, you should operate at the pace necessary for getting your work done, but not the slow pace that allows for daydreaming and internal chatter. Refresh between activities so you can become fully present for each moment of your day. You'll find that taking moments to Refresh pays off by increasing the amount of time you have available for getting things done.

Give yourself points every time you Refresh, and increase the number of daily Refreshes throughout your 90-day Game. Give yourself a point when you alternate Refreshing with increasing your velocity.

Another excellent time to Refresh is when you're feeling a strong emotion or in the midst of a heated exchange with someone. Stop, Refresh, allow your mind to quiet down, and watch how your attitude changes. How often have you regretted speaking or acting out in anger when the simple act of Refreshing would have helped you regain control of your feelings?

By Refreshing, you allow your mind the space and time to present ideas that are more aligned with your higher purpose. So after Refreshing, it's helpful to do what your mind presents immediately, or as soon as you can.

Refresh at the beginning of your meals. I found that when I rushed into eating I'd often overeat. By Refreshing, I had the presence of mind to know when I was full. This happened naturally, and I could stop eating and feel satisfied.

Multitasking

I've discussed multitasking in detail in the chapter "Time," so you may want to reread that section. For The Game, you'll multitask as often as you can to give yourself more velocity. This allows you to accomplish more of your goals, but it also offers you the opportunity to become focused and attentive.

Your body is already a wonderfully efficient multitasking organism as you unconsciously breathe and have any number of bodily functions happening simultaneously. Multitasking creates clarity and focus when you're doing it properly.

I have the ability to read 10,000 words per minute. Many times I've gotten on a stationary bike and instead of letting my thoughts meander, I cycled for 20 minutes and read a complete book of 300 to 500 pages. I noticed that while I read, I intensified my rate of cycling. When I finished the experience of multitasking, I noticed that cycling was easier than before I'd been speed-reading. I'd actually stretched my attention by doing two noncompeting tasks well.

Give yourself points in The Game for multitasking, and for increasing your facility at this skill.

Integration

Integration is related to multitasking. This is a skill for playing The Game in which you find ways to integrate or combine one activity with another.

I found a wonderful way to integrate my goal of doing more spiritual reading every day into my busy travel schedule. I started buying two copies of the book I wanted to read. I tore the pages from one copy and placed them in my suit pockets, briefcase, and various compartments of my luggage. In this way, I could always reach for some pages and read while sitting around during travel delays at airports. At the same time, I had an intact book at home that I could read in the mornings and before bed at night.

Essentially, integration is a skill that helps your life become seamless. Integration allows you to get anything you want done by blending it into other things. I've seen people integrate their desire to stop swearing with saving money or charitable giving. Every time they use profanity, they must put a certain amount of money in a jar. Then they can save the money or donate it to a charity.

Give yourself a point while playing The Game for each time you integrate one activity or action with another. Develop the skill of integrating seamlessly so your life moves as smoothly as a fine ballet.

Speed-reading

During The Game, you're studying yourself and increasing your attention and will. One great skill that you can develop as a means of building focus and discipline is the ability to read thousands of words per minute with comprehension. Can you imagine how much valuable information you could gain by acquiring this skill?

Ken Doyle, a master Game coach with **TheCoachingProgram.com,** says that he used the skill of speed-reading to increase his business acumen. This helped his company considerably increase its earnings. When he'd get into discussions with managers and employees at meetings, Ken would offer a treasure chest of brilliant ideas and suggestions. People were asking him how he knew all these wonderful things, and he told them that he'd taught himself to read 10,000 words per minute. He'd read practically every book available in a short period of time on subjects relating to increasing sales and enhancing customer satisfaction. Because he had such superb comprehension, he was able to teach others how to apply this wisdom profitably.

For every aspect of The Game, there are books, magazines, and other literature you can read to help you achieve your goals. In the past, you've probably accumulated stacks of unread books and magazines on the aspects of life you want to improve, but because you read so slowly, you haven't read them. What if you could increase your speed from the typical 200 to 300 words per minute to the point where you could easily read a book a day, or even an hour? What if you could prove to yourself that speed-reading doesn't decrease comprehension, but improves it by increasing your ability to focus on what you're reading?

Why Read Faster?

I'm going to take you through a series of exercises that I'd like you to practice now and throughout your 90-day Game. Make speed-reading a goal for your entire Game, put it on your To-Be list, and record your reading speed on your Before-and-After displays.

When you're reading the way most people do, you're spending a lot of time processing, free-associating, thinking about the book's content, drifting, and daydreaming. This is why you often reread lines and lose your place. You're not focused. Most of us have reading abilities that are frozen at a third-grade level of maturity, which is where we probably stopped substantively increasing our reading skills.

Before beginning the speed-reading exercises, first do a timed reading. Take any book and turn to a page with straight text; this means a page that doesn't have bullet points or indented quotes. Use a watch with a secondhand to time yourself reading this page for one minute. Now calculate your current reading speed by estimating that a typical book page, which doesn't have teeny-tiny or oversized print, contains approximately 300 words per page. If it took you one minute to read a page, you're reading at about 250 to 300 words per minute. Put this book aside so you can use it to check your speed again later.

Now, prepare yourself and your environment for gaining better focus and attention each time you do the speed-reading exercises below:

- Decrease outside stimulation by turning off the television or any other background noise. You can play some instrumental music if you wish, such as classical or chamber music.

- Sit in a comfortable chair instead of lying down.

- Make sure the room is well ventilated, with plenty of oxygen and bright lights.

- Relax your eyes and Refresh.

- Pick up the book you're going to speed-read and get a sense of it by flipping the pages quickly from front to back. Now you're ready to begin the exercises.

So I can introduce speed-reading exercises to you now, bookmark this page and return to the front of this book. Turn the pages at the rate of one page per second until you're all the way to the end. Don't worry about what you're reading, and don't force yourself to have the *intent* to read. Just keep turning pages. This is called previewing the book. During The Game, I want you to preview every book before you read it, just as you did in this exercise.

Notice how certain words, concepts, and ideas came into your mind during the preview even though you were going through the book quickly. Your comprehension at this point is probably about 5 or 10 percent. You might be operating under the erroneous assumption that had you read slower, you'd have increased your comprehension. It's actually just the opposite. Comprehension is related to focus. The more focused you are, the more you comprehend. Reading faster increases focus. Let's go on to the next exercises, so you can prove this to yourself.

✳ ✳ ✳

More Speed-reading Exercises

Return to the book that you just timed yourself on. Pick another couple of pages with approximately 300 words on them. Now, time yourself again. What did you discover? If you're like most people, you're already reading faster, and you probably caught more words, phrases, and ideas than you did in the first timed exercise.

The second exercise you're going to do is one in which you follow a U or horseshoe-shaped hand stroke as shown in the diagram below.

Speed Reading Strokes

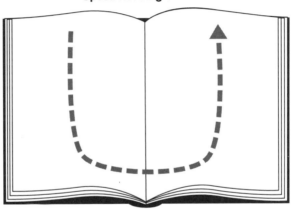

1. Follow your fingers in a U or horseshoe-shaped movement.
One second per page.

Make this stroke across every two pages from the start to finish of this book. Allow one second per page, moving your hand down one page for one second and up the next for a second. In this exercise, you're focusing by following your hand as a pointer. This enables you to see and comprehend more of what the eye is catching as you sweep across the pages.

In the next exercise, you'll use a lazy-S or snakelike hand stroke as shown in the diagram on the next page.

Speed Reading Strokes

1. Follow your fingers in an S or snake-shaped movement.
Two seconds per page.

This time, allow two seconds per page to make the S-stroke. Now, bookmark this page and speed-read from the beginning to the end of this book, using the S-stroke at two seconds per page. How many more ideas are you picking up while reading at this speed?

For the next exercise, you'll use the brush stroke, as shown in the diagram below.

Speed Reading Strokes

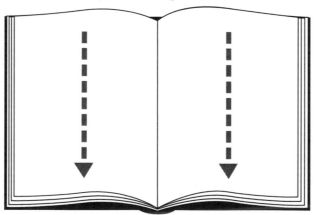

3. Follow your fingers down the center of each page.
Three seconds per page.

With this stroke, your hand is going down the center of each page from the top to the bottom, and you're taking three seconds per page to do it. You're allowing your mind to pick up information through your entire field of vision, including peripheral vision. Now bookmark this page and speed-read this entire book from start to finish using the brush stroke at three seconds per page.

Do the timed reading test once again to rate your speed after you've done the exercises above. I want to congratulate you that at this point—you've read the entire book. You'll have a much deeper grasp of the material because you've done these simple exercises. So take out the book you've been using for timed readings and find another 300-word page. Time yourself for one minute. Again, notice if your comprehension has improved. You speed has probably increased already. Can you imagine what will happen by the end of 90 days after you've frequently practiced these exercises? How exciting for you to have access to a world of books, magazines, and newspapers and read as much as you want on any given subject.

Let's try one more exercise. This is to prove to your mind that you really can comprehend information even while reading faster. For this exercise, you'll need a partner. Take a book you haven't read and open it from the back and turn it upside down. Use the brush stroke, as you did in the last speed-reading exercise. Read upside down and backwards at two to three seconds per page for one minute. Now share with your partner everything you recall about what you read. Aren't you amazed? Look at how much you comprehended even when reading in such an unusual way.

I suggest that once a week you speed-read through this book to find new ideas and to recall key concepts that motivate you and help you focus on your Game.

I'd also like to recommend that you add to your Game using one of the many reputable speed-reading courses available at your local bookstore.

Of course, speed-reading is something you can choose to do or not do. You probably won't want to speed through classic literature that is best read slowly. But you might even want to preview those books so that you'll develop better overall comprehension.

Give yourself points every time you do speed-reading exercises during The Game. Calculate how many books you typically read in a month or week. Give yourself points for every book over that number that you speed-read during The Game.

Each of the skills I've asked you to acquire and improve while playing The Game develops your attention and helps you cut through the tendency to daydream through your life. In the next chapter, you'll learn a couple of fun and highly effective techniques for waking yourself up and getting into action.

✷ ✷ ✷

CHAPTER 26

Consequences and Deadlines

If you're committed to giving yourself rewards for progressing toward your goals, and you combine this practice with consequences for not playing The Game for 90 days, that's all you'll need to make your life happen. Most people only get spurred into action after they've had to pay a consequence. By the time they're faced with a divorce, ill health, or some other unpleasant consequence, it's too late. In The Game, you're going to set up consequences for *yourself*. The more unwilling you are to pay them, the more powerful your Game will be.

What would you be unwilling to suffer for not playing The Game for 90 days? Think of a really embarrassing, funny, and totally unthinkable consequence that won't harm you or anyone else, and write it in your Game journal. Be sure to tell your communities what this consequence is so people can remind you that you definitely don't want to have to do it. Now you have no option but to keep playing The Game in order to achieve your goals.

Begin this process right now by establishing a start date for your Game. Give yourself a consequence if you delay this start date to "someday" or "later." After you've been playing the Game for a while, if you stop for any reason, begin again.

As long as you get back on that horse and ride it, you won't have to administer your consequence. But notice if this is a pattern for you, and take it as coaching. Are you someone who often starts projects but bogs down in the middle and gives up?

Examples of Consequences

I've given you suggestions for consequences in Part II of this book for each aspect of life. Here are a few more you can use as models. People in our coaching program have devised most of these with excellent results.

- If I'm not dating in 90 days, I'll start a dating and matchmaking service for others.

- If I don't play The Game for 90 days, I have to stand on the street corner and sing out loud.

- If I stop playing The Game, I'll wear a pink tutu in public.

- If I don't lose the weight I said I would by a certain date, I'll pay $100 to my partner for every day and every pound I'm over my goal weight.

- If I don't go to my Alcoholics Anonymous meetings, I'll introduce myself to strangers by saying, "Hi, I'm (name). I drink too much, and I know I shouldn't."

- If I don't finish my 90-day Game, I'll go running while wearing a T-shirt that says, "I failed at my destiny, and I'm a loser."

- If I don't finish playing The Game, I'll give each person in my communities a potted plant with the message that says, "I've wasted my life and haven't used the resources God has given me."

Be creative with your consequences, and make them specific to you. Then have fun avoiding them by winning your life.

Deadlines

In The Game, establishing deadlines is more important than having a detailed plan in place. If you have a deadline, you'll make a plan and figure out the details. Of course, the ultimate deadline is death, but since we don't know when that will be, we can decide how we'll be able to die without regrets. A deadline is a commitment for the future that alters how you're behaving now.

Imagine if the IRS said you could pay your taxes whenever you want, and there was no deadline for them. How many taxes do you think they'd be collecting? Right now, we tend to motivate ourselves with deadlines such as retirement, graduation from school, or when the new baby is due. These are valuable, but why not use the power of deadlines to propel you into action in The Game and in life?

Think about what you accomplish during the week before you're leaving for a vacation. This deadline inspires you to become very productive. What if you were this efficient all the time? How much would you accomplish? How much more money would you make?

For The Game, which has a built-in deadline of 90 days, break your goals and the habits you want to acquire or eliminate into smaller pieces with monthly and weekly deadlines. Add consequences and rewards to these deadlines and you're certain to stay on track.

Getting Creative with Deadlines

When you have a deadline, it causes you to become very creative and inventive. Without a deadline, you wait for the ideal circumstances to finish things, and of course, the ideal time never occurs. Deadlines generate velocity. Start doing a countdown around anything you're procrastinating about doing and watch yourself get moving.

Communicate your self-imposed deadlines to your community so you can gain their support in meeting them. For example, what if you talked to your boss, and instead of asking for a raise, you said, "I'm willing to increase my productivity by X amount in 90 days. If I do that, will you be willing to give me a raise or promotion?" Wouldn't he or she be more likely to strike that kind of bargain than the one you'd get by whining that you're not making enough money? In our coaching program, one man used deadlines to increase his income by 1,000 percent, and he was already earning six figures a year!

If you work all the time, could you set a deadline for when you'll take a vacation? Would your mind immediately jump on how to reorganize and prioritize so you could meet that deadline, especially if you had a consequence for *not* taking the vacation?

In most cases, without a deadline, your mind won't create a plan. This is just the way human nature operates. So use The Game's technology to stop your "someday" and "later" games. There's no getting ready to play. Just do it now. This is how you'll fulfill all your dreams.

Having a Game-partner, coach, and mentor will help make your Game the high-quality, unforgettable experience it's meant to be. You'll find out more about this important element of The Game's technology in the next chapter.

✷ ✷ ✷

✦ CHAPTER 27 ✦

Partners and Coaching

Every single relationship in my life has been enhanced dramatically by what I've learned from my partners while playing The Game. As with other games in life, you need a coach to help you through the rough spots.

When you play The Game, you'll select a partner, and the two of you will coach each other every day. With a partner, you'll gain an effective method for keeping up your momentum, not to mention that it's a lot more fun to take this journey with another human being. The time you spend talking with your Game partner is doing an *A Activity* with an *A Relationship*.

The most effective Game partnerships involve competition and cooperation. Each person is helping the other do his or her very best. They will win as a team and rejoice in each other's successes. Venus and Serena Williams, the tennis-playing sisters, are an example of this kind of partnership. Even though the two are fierce competitors on court, they claim to have no sibling rivalry. They say that they think of tennis as a game played within the framework of their relationship, which will last for life.

If you want to know what will really help you win your Game, get focused on what it's going to take to have your partner accomplish goals. The better your partner plays, the more it's going to push and inspire *you*. Partner competition is healthy and fun. One time I was really dragging in my Game, and my partner said, "You can't go to bed tonight without scoring an additional 200 points." We agreed to compete for that mini-goal deadline. That night I accomplished so many things before I went to bed that I felt totally energized, and ended up going to sleep with a strong sense of satisfaction.

Remember that you'll submit your essay at the end of 90 days with your partner, and you'll be judged as a team on whether you can become finalists in The Game I'm sponsoring. One man in **TheCoachingProgram.com** learned an important lesson about his partnering relationship. In our program, the class votes on the winner of the Game. This man had scored the most points, but he hadn't consistently helped his partner win or play The Game. Consequently, the class didn't vote for him as the winner. This was a tough but valuable lesson for him to learn about balancing competition and cooperation in relationships.

Selecting a Partner

Now that you've formulated an initial statement of higher purpose and have selected the aspects of life you most want to improve in 90 days, think about what person would be your best coach for achieving your goals. This should be someone you believe is adept at those things you want to accomplish. The ideal partner brings something to the equation that you don't have, but which you do aspire to. So don't pick a partner who is as inept as you are at those things you want to accomplish.

As I mentioned earlier in this book, a partner doesn't need to be your friend. In fact, I discourage you from combining friendship and partnership for The Game. If your partner is your friend, distinguish between socializing and coaching each other for The Game. Friends often support your weaknesses and join you in gossiping and complaining. This is not the relationship you want with your Game partner.

A partner is someone whom you can trust to help hold you accountable, and who will stand up for the commitments you've made to fulfill your higher purpose. You want a partner who sincerely wants to play The Game with you and who isn't frivolous. This person should also have something at stake and want to win his or her life in 90 days.

Ask yourself what this person could and would do to support you. Your partner needs to be someone you trust as a coach and whose advice you'll respect. Game-players make a commitment to support their partners' higher purpose and help them achieve goals. Partners are anchors, models, mentors, and coaches who deliver that "Go, team, go!" speech we all need to hear.

Partners and Relationships

The Game is a microcosm of your life. It holds a mirror up to you and your relationships. The communication challenges you'll face with your partner are the same you'll find in every other relationship in your life. This is because you're selecting these people to be in your world. So, your partner offers a golden opportunity to resolve issues that you're having with everyone who's important to you.

Personal relationships don't always function well, because two people get together for the purpose of finding happiness. What they really want is for the other person to make them happy. I'm sure you've come to realize that it doesn't work this way. The Game partners are committed to a higher purpose and to helping each other fulfill that purpose. This gives them goals beyond their personal happiness and makes the relationship more satisfying than most partnerships.

One thing I've noticed with all the partners I've seen play The Game over the years is that after they settled into their Games, it was clear that they were perfect for each other. So don't try to use your partner as an excuse for failing or slowing down. Once you start The Game, know that you have the right partner. You've partnered with exactly the person you needed for learning important life lessons.

Calling Your Partner

The rule for The Game is that after you and a partner have selected each other, you need to be in contact with one another by phone every day for about ten minutes. These calls are limited, so you'll get right down to the business at hand and not spend time chit-chatting. In your daily call, you'll be learning how to communicate with another person in a very profound and effective way, so the two of you can offer each other maximum coaching. You'll also need to heed The Game's basic rule of no gossiping and keeping your coaching-call contents confidential. Give yourself points for keeping commitments to your partner each day.

At the beginning and end of each partner call, Refresh. With each call, ask the following questions of each other:

- What commitments weren't you able to keep today?
- Where did you fall short of your goals today?
- How many points did you score today?
- What kind of help or encouragement can I give you today?

Before you end the call, set up the exact time you'll be making your next one, and decide who will be placing it.

Coaches

A member of our coaching program classes (whom I'll call Danny) discovered he had liver cancer. He asked a 70-year-old man, George Page, a friend he'd made in his **Coaching-Program.com** classes, to coach him through the experience of his cancer diagnosis. Doctors had predicted that Danny had only six to twelve months to live.

George had never expected that he could become a coach for someone, but he was exactly the right person for Danny to ask. You see, George had had cancer himself at one time.

George says:

> *My wife and I were visiting Danny and his family. When I was getting ready to go home, Danny asked everybody to leave the room so he could talk to me privately. When we were alone, he said, "I want to beat this thing. Will you coach me?"*
>
> *I'd been feeling reluctant to say too much to Danny about the cancer, but when he asked for my help, I started telling him my thoughts. I talked to him about diet, meditation, healing, balance, and the importance of family—all the things that helped me. I don't know where this advice came from because I have no background in coaching, but Danny and I have talked daily since that first night. Since then, he and I have each been growing phenomenally.*
>
> *Because any of us can die tomorrow, I told Danny that it's important to live each day fully so that when he looks back, he'll know he lived in the best way possible. Since Danny has three little kids, I said that I didn't think he should spend his days fighting cancer and nothing else. The approach we agreed on was for Danny to stay involved in his business and train his wife to take it over.*
>
> *Then I proposed an idea that Danny and his wife both liked. I said, "We have to keep on track here. Why don't we all play The Game again?" Soon, we had completed the lists*

of our goals for playing The Game with the understanding that the rules we made for ourselves could be changed at a moment's notice.

Danny and I expect that he's going to beat the odds that the doctors gave him. He's not accepting the 6- to 12-month prediction, and neither am I. With these expectations, we're seeing a miracle a day with him. He's been able to use his community to contact the finest doctors and healers all over the country. He's balancing his life with a change in diet. After playing The Game the first time, Danny had learned to read 1,000 words a minute, so he's been reading extensively about cancer and chemotherapy. He's working in harmony with himself and going for maximum health. At the same time, he's going to lead the best life possible for as long as he can.

✻ ✻ ✻

Isn't George and Danny's story powerful and enormously inspiring? Here's a man who has been told he may only have six months to live, and he decides to play The Game so that he can make the best use of the time he has left in this world. Can you see now why I'm so committed to showing you how this technology can change your life?

Help from Our Website

TheGameInteractive.com Website is an arena where you can get help finding a partner who wants to play The Game in your local area. We'll also be certifying coaches in the aspects of life you've chosen for your Game. You'll be able to visit the Website to find out who in your area or across the country is a specialist in helping people achieve the goals you want to accomplish.

We'll also increase your coaching resources by posting articles and tips from our coaching-program master instructors and students. You'll have the advantage and support of a worldwide community just by regularly visiting the Website.

Now it's time to get ready to play The Game. Ready, set, organize, go!

✴ ✴ ✴

★ CHAPTER 28 ★

Organizing to
Play The Game

Have you noticed that most people aren't organized enough to produce the results they want in their lives? As you play The Game, your organizational skills will grow because you'll be finding moments where you can score points and accomplish goals on your To-Be and Not-To-Be lists. Prior to playing The Game, you can use The Game Plan below to help you work your way, step-by-step, toward committing to your Game start date.

When you look at how much you've accomplished in your life so far, it's going to be fun to imagine what could be possible when you really get organized. You're going to be absolutely amazing! Or maybe you'll be like children. Bill Meyer says, "I was watching my six-year-old at the McDonald's playground. Within two minutes, he and another little boy had introduced themselves to each other and had developed rules for a variation of hide-and-seek. Poof! They were off to play their game. Why do adults have so much trouble getting organized?"

The very nature of The Game requires planning instead of thinking or daydreaming. It's an exercise in managing and clarifying your own expectations so you're prepared to fulfill them. You might think that getting organized to play The Game looks like a lot to do. It is. This Game is an attempt to kick-start a life that has been stalling, to bring you out of the sidelines . . . to get you off the bench.

Share Your Ideas with Others

How often have you jumped into something without preparation, only to lose velocity and become confused, disorganized, and harried? Because The Game is designed to overwhelm you as you play to win, so you'll want to have every advantage before you begin. Then, no matter what comes up while you're playing, you know that you'll have the time and energy to deal with it. This isn't a game you're playing to lose.

When I've prepared to play The Game, I've allotted several hours to focus on gathering materials and preparing my strategy as if I was preparing to launch a rocket. I know that after this rocket of The Game takes off, if anything is missing, I'll have to handle it along the way. And I will. And you will, too. So don't fret about having everything lined up perfectly before you start playing. Just follow The Game Plan checklist below and organize to the best of your ability.

As you find shortcuts and brilliant ideas for preparation, jot them down so you can share them with others at **TheGameInteractive.com** Website. This is the value of networking. You might be thinking that a certain challenge you're having in playing The Game is only happening to you, but there may be 500 people around the world who have found myriad creative ways of dealing with your same issue. You can all learn from each other.

The Game Plan

- Chose a partner, or contact us through our Website at **TheGameInteractive.com** to see who in your area is in The Game and looking for a partner.

- Get a Game Journal. Choose any kind of notebook you'd like to use. Visit our Website for information on how to do your Game Journal online.

- If you did not do the exercises the first time you read through the book, go back now and do them. These should include your Before Display, statement of higher purpose, To-Be and Not-To-Be lists, the lists of tasks and behaviors you'll give yourself points for and deduct points for, and the intermediary deadlines you're setting for achieving goals.

- Get an organizational and time-management system that works for you.

- Create some sort of system or mechanism for keeping track of your points.

- Arrange for a planning and strategy session with your partner to determine and coordinate the aspects of life you'll be working on, as well as the fundamental design of The Game you created.

- Announce your Game and higher purpose to your relevant communities, with all of the necessary information that will enable them to encourage and support you and hold you to your commitments and consequences.

- With your partner, go to our Website and register at **TheGameInteractive.com**, or complete and mail in the registration on the next page to enter The Game contest.

Registering for The Game

You can fill out The Game Registration Form below and mail it to: The Game, P.O. Box 910147, San Diego, CA 92191-0147, USA. You can also go to **TheGameInteractive.com** Website and register online.

First Name:_____ Middle Initial:____ Last Name:_____

Address:_____

City:_____ State:_____ Zip Code:_____

Country:_____E-mail Address:_____

Telephone Number (day):_____(evening):_____

Your Partner's First Name:_____

Your Partner's Middle Initial:_____Your Partner's Last Name:_____

Your Partner's E-mail Address:_____

Your Partner's Address:_____

Your Partner's City: _____State:_____Zip Code:_____

Your Partner's Country:_____Your Partner's E-mail Address:_____

Your Partner's Telephone Number (day):_____(evening):_____

The Aspects of Life You Have Selected:

1._____

2._____

3._____

4._____

5._____

The Aspects of Life Your Partner Has Selected:

1._____

2._____

3._____

4._____

5._____

Optional Information So We May Better Serve You:

Your Sex: ❏ Male ❏ Female   Your Age:_____ Your Kind of Computer: ❏ PC ❏ Mac

Your Kind of Operating System: ❏ Mac ❏ Windows 2000/Windows ❏ ME/Windows 95

Your Kind of ISP: ❏ AOL ❏ Internet Explorer ❏ Netscape

Your Kind of Connection: ❏ 56K ❏ DSL ❏ Cable Modem

Your Kind of Wireless Communication Device:

Your Cell Phone:_____ PDA: _____ Beeper:_____

Your Income Range (circle one):

      0–$25,000 $25,000–50,000 $50,000–100,000
      $100,000–250,000   Above $250,000

Your Occupation:_____

Where or How You Purchased This Book:_____

Number of Books You Purchased:_____

Optional Information about Your Partner So We May Better Serve You:

Your Partner's Sex: ❏ Male ❏ Female

Your Partner's Age:_____

Your Partner's Kind of Computer: ❏ PC ❏ Mac

Your Partner's Kind of Operating System:

      ❏ Mac   ❏ Windows 2000/Windows   ❏ ME/Windows 95

Your Partner's Kind of ISP: ❏ AOL ❏ Internet Explorer ❏ Netscape

Your Partner's Kind of Connection: ❏ 56K ❏ DSL ❏ Cable Modem

Your Partner's Kind of Wireless Communication Device:

Your Partner's Cell Phone:_____ PDA:_____ Beeper:_____

Your Partner's Income Range (circle one):

      0–$25,000 $25,000–50,000 $50,000–100,000
      $100,000–250,000   Above $250,000

Your Partner's Occupation:_____

Where or How Your Partner Purchased the Book:_____

Number of Books Your Partner Purchased:_____

Congratulations! You are and your partner are now registered in The Game contest!

* * *

Some Words of Wisdom from Other Game-Players

"Take seriously the advice to drop all self-criticism. It's a game, just a game. To add the would-haves and should-haves and if-onlys to your Game will keep you from seeing the point of playing it. You'll become your own worst enemy. Get over yourself. Have some fun!"

— **Bill Meyer**

"I tend not to think of life as a game. [Memo to self: Get a sense of humor.] Life is a serious business. [Memo to self: Get a life and then decide. Also: See previous memo to self.] There are parts of the program I'm just not going to do! [Memo to self: So, they should change what works for others just for you? Stuff you don't want to do, don't do. Figure out why you're resisting it; then, if you still don't want to do it, don't!]"

— **Matt Whalen**

"Really go for it. Don't hold back. Give it your all. If you cheat, cheat well."

— **Ken Doyle**

"You have to give The Game 100 percent and not play it halfway. It's a matter of giving of yourself, which I was willing to do, so I got a heck of a lot out of it."

— **Orville Lerch**

"My one piece of advice is if you are reading this book and it speaks to you, reread it and reread it again. Repetition is the mother of excellence."

— **Timothy Bellars**

"Don't think. Stop whining; stop making excuses that this isn't possible for you or that your issues are too big for this. These aren't difficult concepts. They're easy to grasp. There's not a certain religious orientation to The Game, and it isn't too technical. You don't need to be skilled to play it. You don't have to be an athlete. You just have to be a person who is willing and has the desire to move ahead and overcome a lot of the obstacles that are holding you back."

— **Greg Kadet**

✱ ✱ ✱

"Stop trying to figure out The Game, and just play it!"
— **Sarano Kelley**

✱ ✱ ✱

★ EPILOGUE ★

I want to congratulate you for being such an extraordinary human being. How many times have you bought books and never completed them? The fact that you've read this entire book tells me that you truly understand that your life is important.

I want to encourage you to take the next steps and go from reading the book as a spectator to becoming a Player. You'll be taking your life and the lives of people around you to a whole new level.

This book is an incredible journey, but at the same time, it's only a two-dimensional experience compared to the multi-dimensional opportunities at our **GameInteractive.com** Website. The site is meant to be a Game in itself and leads you through the experience of building a new sense of structure, affinity, community, and skills that will last you a lifetime. The Website is a place of constant renewal in your quest to lead a more fulfilling life.

TheGameInteractive.com also represents a very important structure, because you can keep track of your entire Game on our site. You can use it as your journal and allow it to walk you through the building of your Game. Now you can see why

I've encouraged you to become familiar with the Internet—there is so much you can take advantage of once you log on.

The Game creates its own community because on **TheGameInteractive.com,** you can chat with our master Game coaches, see live broadcasts of Game classes, and communicate with other Game-player partners in your area. It also lets you know when I'll be leading The Game in your part of the world.

Dr. Martin Kettelhut and I have trained and certified coaches who are listed on **TheGameInteractive.com** Website. These Game-masters are certified coaches and master players who can assist you in their field of expertise and show you how to use The Game's technology with whatever system or philosophy they've developed. We're very proud of our association with them and are constantly reviewing the results they produce and the feedback from you to continue to upgrade their certification.

I'm offering a special invitation for you as a follow-up to reading this book and playing The Game. As I mentioned earlier, **TheCoachingProgram.com** offers a 15-month elite coaching program for people who want to make a difference in this world and in their own personal lives. The Website incorporates six principles for having anything you want in your life: training, practice, coaching, affinity, structure, and community.

If you want to attain the life of your dreams, I suggest that you register for **TheCoachingProgram.com.** You'll be teamed up with a high-powered group of individuals who meet once every 90 days and receive daily accountability and weekly coaching from master Game coaches. The outstanding quotes and inspiring stories in this book came from **TheCoachingProgram.com's** many clients who have played The Game and won their lives.

In addition, **TheCoachingProgram.com** is offering two specially designed seminars to help you continue your momentum and progress, or enhance your experience of The Game.

These seminars are:

- *"Win Your Life in 90 Days,"* a two-weekend seminar in which you'll play The Game with the help of a highly motivated group of other Game-players and return in three months to discuss results and expand your horizons.

- *"Double Your Business Workshop,"* a two-day seminar with follow-up consulting designed to increase income for financial professionals and sales people who have a recurring client base.

To register for these seminars and get more information about **TheCoachingProgam.com**, e-mail us at: **info@thecoachingprogram.com** or visit our Website at: **www.TheCoachingProgram.com**.

✳ ✳ ✳

Welcome to The Game. I'll look forward to seeing proof of what I already know—*you are an incredible human being!*
Now, Refresh.
Let the Renaissance begin in earnest!

✳ ✳ ✳

Sarano Kelley grew up in a gang-infested neighborhood in Brownsville, New York, and became a Vassar College graduate who was earning $400,000 in commission as a stockbroker on Wall Street by the time he was 23 years old.

When he was at the height of success as a stockbroker, he had a life-changing experience—he lost some of his beloved family members in a fire. This tragedy caused him to begin a spiritual and philosophical journey to understand the meaning and purpose of his life.

Sarano is now a motivational speaker and life coach who has trained more than 250,000 people. He served as a media coach for leading corporate and government spokespersons who were being interviewed on *CNN*, *20/20*, and *60 Minutes;* and for President Clinton's White House Fellows, a leadership group that included General Colin Powell.

Sarano has been a trainer and consultant for the elite Hanover Forum producers at Kidder Peabody, a top Wall Street firm, and for leading producers at Paine Webber. As the corporate spokesman for Phoenix Investment Partners, a $50 billion financial institution, he addressed 50,000 people annually. He travels extensively, both domestically and internationally, and is often invited to give keynote speeches for Fortune 500 companies.

Sarano is founder of The Center for Excellence and **The-CoachingProgram.com,** both of which are exploring opportunities to go public on the stock market with the launch of his book, *The Game*, and his Website, **TheGameInteractive.com.**

★ ★ ★

Other Jodere Group Titles

✳ ✳ ✳

Crossing Over, by John Edward (available August 2001)

What If God Were the Sun? a novel by John Edward

You Can Find Anybody!
and *When in Doubt, Check Him Out,*
both by Joseph Culligan, Licensed Private Investigator

✳ ✳ ✳

All of the above are available at your local bookstore,
by calling **Jodere Group, Inc.,** at **(800) 569-1002,**
or by contacting the Jodere Group distributor:
Hay House, Inc., at **(760) 431-7695** or **(800) 654-5126**

★ NOTES ★

★ Notes ★

✷ ✷ ✷

We hope you enjoyed this Jodere Group book.
If you would like additional information
about Jodere Group, Inc., please contact:

Jodere Group, Inc.
P.O. Box 910147
San Diego, CA 92191-0147
(800) 569-1002

✷ ✷ ✷

Distributed in the United States by:

Hay House, Inc.
P.O. Box 5100
Carlsbad, CA 92018-5100
(760) 431-7695 or (800) 654-5126
(760) 431-6948 (fax) or (800) 650-5115 (fax)
www.hayhouse.com

✷ ✷ ✷